# MASTERSON
# and
# ROOSEVELT

## by

## Jack DeMattos

## THE EARLY WEST SERIES

CREATIVE PUBLISHING COMPANY
BOX 9292, PHONE 409-775-6047
COLLEGE STATION, TEXAS 77840

THE
EARLY WEST

DeMattos, Jack, 1944—
    Masterson and Roosevelt.

    (The Early West Series)
    Bibliography: p.
    Includes index.
    1. Masterson, Bat 1853-1921—Friends and associates.
2. Masterson, Bat, 1853-1921—Homes—New York (N.Y.)
3. Roosevelt, Theodore, 1858-1919—Friends and
associates. 4. Roosevelt, Theodore, 1858-1919—Homes—New
York (N.Y.) 5. Peace officers—West (U.S.)—Biography.
6. United States marshals—Biography. 7. Journalists—
New York (N.Y.)—Biography. I. Title, II. Series.
F595.M35D45 1984   973.91'1'0922   84-17591

    ISBN 0-932702-31-7

Dedicated to

the memory of my father

Anthony DeMattos

October 20,1916 — January 4, 1984

# Contents

# Introduction

One of the residual benefits gained from researching and writing a biography of an historical figure is the opportunity to come to know others who share an interest in the personality. During the course of my study of the life of W. B. "Bat" Masterson which culminated in 1979 in the publication of *Bat Masterson, The Man and the Legend*, I became acquainted with Jack De-Mattos of North Attleboro, Massachusetts, and Jim Earle of College Station, Texas, western history enthusiasts who were intrigued by the career of this legendary gunfighter. DeMattos is an artist and avid researcher who uncovered much new information on the gunfighters' West and has published his findings in numerous magazine articles. Earle, also an artist, is a publisher and collector who owns, among other gunfighter artifacts, the only authenticated sixshooter of the many Masterson purchased and carried during his career.

When I learned that Jack DeMattos had put together the story of Bat Masterson's relationship with Theodore Roosevelt and that Jim Earle was publishing it, I happily agreed to provide an introduction.

This volume goes far in filling a void in the life histories of two fascinating Americans, Bat Masterson and Teddy Roosevelt. The friendship between the two as evidenced by the correspondence presented here has been overlooked, ignored, or barely touched upon by their biographers. It was a friendship born of mutual respect and its revelation provides new insight into an understanding of the character of each.

Masterson's currying of Roosevelt's favor is easily understood. After all, TR in the early years of the twentieth century was a national monument, the hero of San Juan Hill, the holder of a succession of high political offices culminating in his ascendency to the presidency of the United States after the assassination of William McKinley in September of 1901, an educated man of good breeding, vast connections, and great popularity. Access to such a man greatly enhanced Bat's prestige among the denizens of the New York sports, theatrical, and newspaper milieu in which he operated after 1902. It also benefitted him financially when his high-placed friend chose to have him appointed to a well-paid, undemanding federal officer's post in New York. And yet, in spite of the pride, pleasure, and financial gain Masterson derived from his closeness to the president, he could still refuse Roosevelt's invitation to a formal dress function, as DeMattos recounts. Bat held strong opinions on many subjects, including proper attire, and an aging frontiersman in a tuxedo he considered improper, presidential invitation or no.

Not so readily comprehensible is Roosevelt's affinity for a celebrated gunfighter who (albeit undeservedly) had attained national notoriety as the slayer of victims numbering in the dozens. Masterson was a man of humble origins and little formal education who throughout most of his adult years had earned a precarious livelihood as a professional gambler. He had been a close associate and staunch defender of desperate characters and man-killers such as Wyatt Earp and the Thompson brothers, Ben and Bill. Bellicose and contentious, he had been declared *persona non grata* in more than one Western community and forced to leave. Within two weeks of his arrival in New York City after a checkered career in the West he had been arrested on a charge of fleecing a clergyman in a braced gambling game. Roosevelt was sensitive to Masterson's notoriety and its possible effect on his own reputation. In a letter notifying Bat of his appointment as deputy. U. S. Marshal for the Southern District of New York, quoted in this volume, he admonished his friend to behave himself so as not to provide ammunition for Bat's enemies and TR's critics.

But Theodore Roosevelt recognized in Bat Masterson qualities that he himself possessed in abundance and that he greatly admired in others: unyielding resolution, physical courage, forthrightness, steadfast loyalty to friends, patriotism bordering on the fanatic, and rock-bound Republicanism. Despite two decades of lurid newspaper accounts detailing Masterson's sanguinary sixgun encounters, Roosevelt knew that Bat was no killer; he had learned early in his political career that simply because an allegation appears in print, "it ain't necessarily so," a truism just as valid today. Among his many accomplishments, Roosevelt was an historian and author. With his historical perspective he recognized intellectually the importance and uniqueness of the American frontier experience; as a writer he was emotionally affected by the enduring romantic appeal of the Wild West era. Bat Masterson was a frontier adventurer who had helped clear the plains of the buffalo, had fought desperate battles with Indians, and had worn the star of the lawman in remote and uproarious frontier camps where the rule of law was tenuous. Masterson was a man that Roosevelt, even at the peak of his power and popularity, could admire and feel proud to call a friend.

It is an engrossing story, this account of an incongruous relationship between a president and a gunfighter, one that has not been told before. Jack DeMattos was wisely chosen to let the tale unfold in the words of the participants themselves, adding only what explanatory information is necessary for clarification, Read, be enlightened, enjoy.

Robert K. DeArment
Sylvania, Ohio
September, 1984

# Acknowledgements

My most obvious debt is to Bat Masterson and Theodore Roosevelt, whose unusual friendship inspired this first volume of the "White House Gunfighters" trilogy. Next in order are my publishers, Jim and Theresa Earle, who have made it possible to share the story of *The President and the Gunfighter* with you.

Invaluable assistance was provided by Wallace Finley Dailey, curator of the Theodore Roosevelt Collection at Harvard, as well as John D. Forbes, Office Manager of Woodlawn Cemetery in the Bronx, and Eugene R. Schultz, Manager of Frank E. Campbell's Funeral Chapel, Inc. of New York City.

Joseph W. Snell of the Kansas State Historical Society was most generous in sharing his impressive collection of Masterson material, as was Bat's best biographer, Robert K. DeArment of Sylvania, Ohio. Historian Joseph G. Rosa, of England, has been a constant source of information, inspiration and encouragement during this, and numerous other projects. A note of thanks is also due to Ed Doherty, my friend and editor at *Real West*, as well as to historian Glenn G. Boyer, Robert F. Palmquist, William B. Secrest and Al Turner.

For their friendship, suggestions and encouragement I would also like to thank Don Barnes, Cliff Erickson, Helen Garant, Bill Kelly, Cora Masterson Land, Irving Metzman, Dave and June O'Leary, Dick Weatherford as well as people too numerous to mention at both the New York Historical Society and the New York Public Library.

This list would not be complete without mentioning my immediate family—my wife Sandi and our children Dawn and Greg—who have endured my "hobby" of western history, and shared me with a typewriter, longer than either they or I care to remember.

Thank you—one and all,

Jack DeMattos

# Preface

New York City provides the fitting backdrop for most of the events detailed in *Masterson and Roosevelt*. Fitting because of the mutual affection that President Theodore Roosevelt and Bat Masterson both had for the "Big Apple." Theodore Roosevelt was born there on October 27, 1858, at 28 East 20th Street. Although he lived elsewhere most of his life, Roosevelt found excuses to visit his hometown again and again.

Bat Masterson was not born there, but he adopted New York as his "hometown" late in life. Nearly a third of Bat's life was spent as a Manhattan resident. For the final eighteen years of his life, Bat was employed as a sports editor by the New York *Morning Telegraph*. He hobnobbed with many of the leading sports and theatrical figures of his day. He was at the heart of the action, and loved it. Indeed, the only time Bat seemed inclined to leave his Broadway haunts, were those occasions when he was obliged to cover some out-of-town prizefight for his paper.

It seems ironic that what may prove to be the most interesting period in Bat Masterson's life—his New York City years—received barely passing mention from his two biographers. Richard O'Connor's 1957 "biography" of Masterson contained 263 pages—only 34 of which were devoted to Bat's New York City years; Robert K. DeArment's 1979 biography was vastly superior on all counts, and contained 441 pages—yet only 30 of those pages were devoted to the period in question.

The book will shed some new light on those colorful years. It will be told as it happened, by the President and the gunfighter themselves or their contemporaries, in the form of actual letters and newspaper accounts. Most of these documents are appearing here, in book form, for the first time. These various documents form a story that nearly tells itself—with only the most minimal assist from this writer. The story they tell is one that history has thus far overlooked—the story of the unique friendship between *Masterson and Roosevelt.*

**Jack DeMattos**

William Barclay "Bat" Masterson (1853-1921)

# 1

# Deputy U.S. Marshal

Blame it on Alfred Henry Lewis. More than any other man, it was Lewis who gave the world the swashbuckling image it still retains of Bat Masterson. Even though, as we shall see, Masterson himself tried to destroy that image, it has prevailed— growing in intensity with each passing year. Time has enhanced, rather than eroded, the blood-and-thunder image of Bat Masterson as a clear-eyed, straight-shooting, lawman who bears scant resemblance to the pot-bellied New Yorker you'll meet on these pages.

Blame it on the twenty-sixth President of the United States. It was Theodore Roosevelt who took Alfred Henry Lewis up on a not-so-casual suggestion, made during a White House luncheon, and put Bat Masterson on the federal payroll. At the time of his White House visit, Lewis was working on a fictionalized biography of his close friend Bat Masterson, that would eventually appear in book form as *The Sunset Trail*. Lewis' efforts on Bat's behalf hardly ended with book writing. A year earlier he got his brother, William Eugene Lewis, to provide Masterson with employment on a breezy tabloid William was editing called *The Morning Telegraph*.

Roosevelt had met Bat nearly twenty years before in the West and liked him. Still he was reluctant to give him an appointment. Roosevelt's appointment of other gunfighters such as Pat Garrett and Ben Daniels were not well-received, and ended up making political hay for his enemies. The President wasn't at all certain that—with an election approaching—he wanted to give any more ammunition to his political opponents.

The President told Lewis that he would need assurances that Bat could, at least, read and write and not cause him embarrassment by proving to be illiterate. Lewis didn't waste any time.

As soon as he returned to his New York City apartment Lewis made a hasty phone call to Bat Masterson, who was then lavishly ensconced in a suite of rooms at one of Edwardian New York's most colorful hotels—The Delaven, owned by Masterson's close friend Tom O'Rourke. On the same day that he called Bat, Lewis sent this letter to the President:

October 16, 1904

My Dear Mr. President—

Let me thank you for your extreme goodness to me during my stay; also to call your attention to the fact that the education of our homicidal friend has not been neglected. Permit me to enclose a letter.

Very truly yours

ALFRED HENRY LEWIS

The letter Lewis enclosed (a put up job if there ever was one) read as follows:

> The Delaven
> Broadway & Fortieth Street,
> New York
> Tom O'Rourke, Proprietor
> Telephone 1653—38th St.
> 2809—38th St.

Oct 16 1904

My Dear Alfred

Judge Colborn has been waiting to see you further about the book and goes to Washington tonight for that purpose.
I have wired asking you to give him a little of your time.
Really I   beleive (sic) there is a good thing in the book and I hope you see it and take a hand with—the Judge who is  one of my dearest friends and a gentleman who I would endorse for any thing any where to any one &
I sincerely hope he will not miss you

Yours Sincerely

W. B. MASTERSON

The letters had the desired effect—but being a shrewd politician, Roosevelt decided to delay the Masterson appointment until after election day. On November 8, 1904 Theodore Roosevelt (who had been filling out the term of the assassinated William McKinley) became President in his own right by defeating his Democratic opponent by a vote of 7,623,486 to 5,007,911.

One of President Roosevelt's first acts after his election was to find a federal appointment for Bat Masterson. According to the most repeated version, Roosevelt invited Bat to the White House and informed him that the appointment of United States Marshal for Oklahoma was his for the asking. Unfortunately, Bat had had it with the West and had no desire to return. He wanted to remain where the action was—New York City.

At this point something must be said—absolutely NO evidence of this offer exists in the form of an extant letter or document. The only sources for this story are an interview with Bat, published by the New York *Times* on April 2, 1905 (which appears later in this book), and the introduction Alfred Henry Lewis wrote for a series of articles by Bat in the January, 1907 issue of *Human Life*. The Lewis introduction read as follows:

> . . . Mr. Masterson is no longer a queller of "bad men," but a resident of New York and a contributor to the press. Also he is a warm personal friend of President Roosevelt, who caused him to be named a Deputy United States Marshal for the southern district of New York.
>
> President Roosevelt, following his election, was for naming Mr. Masterson marshal of the Indian Territory. The place has twice the salary of the one he holds and carries with it the naming of twenty-two deputies, and yet Mr. Masterson declined it.

*Bat Masterson as he looked in 1885 at the age of thirty-two when he first met Theodore Roosevelt. (DeMattos Collection)*

"It wouldn't do," he said. "The man of my peculiar reputation couldn't hold such a place without trouble. If I were to go out to the Indian Territory as marshal I can see what would happen. I'd have some drunken boy to kill once a year. Some kid who was born after I took my guns off would get drunk and look me over; and the longer he looked the less he'd be able to see where my reputation came from. In the end he'd crawl round to a gun play and I'd have to send him over the jump.

"Almost any other man could hold the office and never see a moment's trouble. But I couldn't; my record would prove a never-failing bait to the dime-novel reading youngsters, locoed to distinguish themselves and make a fire-eating reputation, and I'd have to bump 'em off.

"So, Mr. President, with all thanks to you, I believe I won't take the place. I've finally got out of that zone of fire and I hope never to go back to it."

It was then President Roosevelt did the next best thing, and caused Mr. Masterson's appointment as a Deputy Marshal in New York.

This "next best thing" didn't just happen. Pressure (presumably from the President) was put upon United States Marshal William Henkel, of the Southern District of New York, to take Bat Masterson on as a deputy. As a result of the high-pressured efforts in Bat's behalf, Henkel finally sent this letter to William H. Moody, the Attorney General of the United States:

Department of Justice,
Office of the United States Marshal,
Southern District of New York,
United States Court-House,
Room 56, Third Floor.


New York, January 26th, 1905

The Attorney General, U.S,
Washington, D.C.

Dear Sir:

I respectfully request the authority to appoint an additional Office Deputy U.S. Marshal, at a salary not exceeding $2000 per annum.

My reasons for making this request are based on the fact, that the business of this office has vastly increased over former years and the present force is inadequate to handle it and at the same time, meet certain demands that are made from time to time for help from the office of the U.S. Attorney. For instance in the Slocum disaster; the Cohen and Rosenthal silk fraud case and the recent wholesale violation of the naturalization laws, he was compelled to ask for additional help from the Department, to assist in collecting evidence.

If you concede this authority to appoint, it is my intention to detail the new appointee to the U.S. Attorney's office, to be under his personal supervision and instruction and also to take charge of the Grand Jury room when that body is in session—at present it is often necessary to take a deputy from some other important duty for this latter work. In former years it was customary to detail a deputy to this post, but on my assuming office, I was compelled to take him away and assign him to work created by the new Bankruptcy law.

The gentleman I desire to recommend for appointment as Office Deputy U.S. Marshal, is W.B. Masterson, a resident of this City, most highly endorsed and in every way worthy to fill this office in a most creditable manner.

Awaiting your early reply, I am

Yours respectfully,

WILLIAM HENKEL

U.S. Marshal

Bat's appointment went through with no strings; the only minor complication was caused by Bat himself. Since he probably didn't expect the appointment to go through so quickly, Bat took his wife Emma for a vacation in Hot Springs, Arkansas. While in Hot Springs this letter from the President was forwarded to Bat:

February 2, 1905

Mr. W.B. Masterson,
The Delavan,
Broadway and Fortieth Street,
New York, N.Y.

Dear Bat:

It was a pleasure to get you the appointment as Deputy Marshal. Now you have doubtless seen that there has been a good deal of hostile comment upon it in the press. I do not care a snap of my fingers for this; but I do care very much that you shall not by any act of yours seem to justify this criticism.

I want you not only to be a vigilant, courteous and efficient officer, always on hand, always polite to every one, always ready for any duty that comes up, but I also want you to carry yourself so that no one can find in any action of yours cause for scandal or complaint.

You must be careful not to gamble or do anything while you are a public officer which might afford opportunity to your enemies and my critics to say that your appointment was improper.

I wish you would show this letter to Alfred Henry Lewis and go over the matter with him.

Sincerely yours,

THEODORE ROOSEVELT

Bat took both the Presidential appointment—and lecture— in stride. He saw no reason to cut short his Hot Springs vacation simply to rush back to New York for the formality of a swearing-in ceremony, and managed to hang around the resort another seven weeks. The news media wasn't as laid-back about the matter; even the prestigious New York *Times* gave the Masterson appointment prominent coverage on page 2 of their issue for Tuesday, Feb. 7, 1905:

## ROOSEVELT GETS JOB FOR BAT MASTERSON

Good Bad-Man Appointed a Deputy Marshal Here.

### PERSONAL REQUEST DID IT

Westerner Has Long Record as Dead Shot and Killer of
Sure-Thing Gamblers.

WASHINGTON, Feb. 6—William B. Masterson was appointed Deputy United States Marshal by Marshal William Henkel of the Southern District of New York on the personal request of President Roosevelt, who has known Mr. Masterson for several years, and believes that he is a good man for the place.

"Bat" Masterson is to be a Deputy United States Marshal in New York, under command of Marshal Henkel, just as soon as the ex-Sheriff of Western communities can reach New York from Hot Springs, Ark. The soft-spoken man from the West, who has won and worn the reputation of being a good "bad man," was appointed to a vacancy in the service through the solicitation of President Roosevelt, who has had a personal fondness for the man since the time when Mr. Roosevelt was an amateur ranchman in the Wild West.

"Bat" Masterson is of the strenuous order, and since he gave up killing for the sake of orderly government has been a constant attendant at all the greater prizefights that have taken place in the United States since the appearance of John L. Sullivan.

'Mr. Masterson,' said Marshal Henkel yesterday, 'was recommended to me by some of the best men of the country—men of importance in National life. He is a capable

# ROOSEVELT GETS JOB FOR BAT MASTERSON

## Good Bad-Man Appointed a Deputy Marshal Here.

## PERSONAL REQUEST DID IT

### Westerner Has Long Record as Dead Shot and Killer of Sure-Thing Gamblers.

WASHINGTON, Feb. 6.—William R. Masterson was appointed Deputy United States Marshal by Marshal Henkel of the Southern District of New York on the personal request of President Roosevelt, who has known Mr. Masterson for several years, and believes that he is a good man for the place.

"Bat" Masterson is to be a Deputy United States Marshal in New York, under command of Marshal Henkel, just as soon as the ex-Sheriff of Western communities can reach New York from Hot Springs, Ark. The soft-spoken man from the West, who has won and worn the reputation of being a good "bad man," was appointed to a vacancy in the service through the solicitation of President Roosevelt, who has had a personal fondness for the man since the time when Mr. Roosevelt was an amateur ranchman in the Wild West. "Bat" Masterson is of the strenuous order, and since he gave up killing for the sake of orderly government has been a constant attendant at all the greater prizefights that have taken place in the United States since the appearance of John L. Sullivan.

"Mr. Masterson," said Marshal Henkel yesterday, "was recommended to me by some of the best men of the country—men of importance in National life. He is a capable man and will make an efficient Deputy Marshal. The appointment was made last week, and all that remains to make it effective is for the new deputy to walk into this office and take the oath."

"Bat" Masterson is credited with having killed a score of men while making Western towns orderly. Among the many of his exploits was the slaying of four men who had killed his brother, a peace officer. Masterson never talks of these affairs, except to say that he never harmed any man except in the discharge of his duty.

Masterson was once a Deputy United States Marshal at Denver. Before that he was Town Marshal at Dodge City, and later Sheriff of the county of which that place is the seat. He succeeded in ridding the town of "sure-thing" gamblers, after a running fight of several weeks. In that time he killed a dozen or more lawless characters, and his reputation as a sure shot was spread widely. He came to New York in the Fall of 1888, at the request of ex-Superintendent of Police Thomas Byrnes. George Gould had been receiving a number of threatening anonymous letters. At first Mr. Gould paid no attention to the communications, but when handwriting experts declared them to have been written by an insane man, Mr. Gould decided it would be well to have some one to look out for the writer, who promised to shoot Mr. Gould at sight. Superintendent Byrnes told Mr. Gould that he needed some man who wouldn't be afraid to shoot up Broadway even during the busy hours of the day, if necessary, and who would hit the man shot at, and not some other unfortunate individual.

Superintendent Byrnes then suggested Masterson, and "Bat" came on from Denver, bringing his wife and family here. For eight months the Westerner followed Mr. Gould like a shadow, until the writer of the letters was finally caught at the residence of Miss Helen Gould, who he insisted had promised to marry him.

Since that time Masterson has made his headquarters in New York, spending the greater part of his time here. He has been employed at the race tracks by bookmakers, who thought it a good insurance to have Masterson handy in case of trouble.

*A clipping from the New York TIMES of February 7, 1905, page 2, column 2. (Jack DeMattos Collection.)*

man and will make an efficient Deputy Marshal. The appointment was made last week, and all that remains to make it effective is for the new deputy to walk into this office and take the oath.'

"Bat" Masterson is credited with having killed a score of men while making Western towns orderly. Among the many of his exploits was the slaying of four men who had killed his brother, a peace officer. Masterson never talks of these affairs, except to say that he never harmed any man except in the discharge of his duty.

Masterson was once a Deputy United States Marshal at Denver. Before that he was Town Marshal at Dodge City, and later Sheriff of the county of which that place is the seat. He succeeded in ridding the town of "sure-thing" gamblers, after a running fight of several weeks. In that time he killed a dozen or so more lawless characters, and his reputation as a sure shot was spread widely.

He came to New York in the Fall of 1893, at the request of ex-Superintendent of Police Thomas Byrnes. George Gould had been receiving a number of threatening anonymous letters. At first Mr. Gould paid no attention to the communications, but when handwriting experts declared them to have been written by an insane man, Mr. Gould decided it would be well to have some one look out for the writer, who promised to shoot Mr. Gould on sight. Superintendent Byrnes told Mr. Gould that he needed some man who wouldn't be afraid to shoot up Broadway even during the busy hours of the day, if necessary, and who would hit the man shot at, and not some other unfortunate individual.

Superintendent Byrnes then suggested Masterson, and "Bat" came on from Denver, bringing his wife and family here. For eight months the Westerner followed Mr. Gould like a shadow, until the writer of the letters was finally

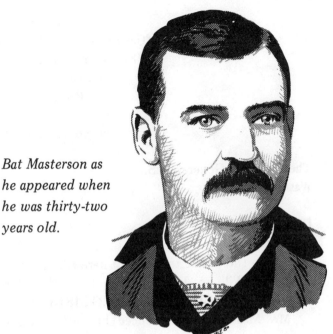

*Bat Masterson as he appeared when he was thirty-two years old.*

caught at the residence of Miss Helen Gould, who he insisted had promised to marry him.

Since that time Masterson has made his headquarters in New York, spending the greater part of his time here. He has been employed at the race tracks by bookmakers, who thought it good insurance to have Masterson handy in case of trouble.

Finally, Bat returned from his vacation in Hot Springs, and at 3 o'clock on the afternoon of Tuesday, March 28, 1905 went through the formality of his swearing-in ceremony. For the official record, this letter was transmitted to Attorney General William H. Moody:

Department of Justice,
Office of the United States Marshal,
Southern District of New York,
United States Court-House,
Room 56, Third Floor.

New York, March 28th, 1905

The Attorney General, U.S.,
Washington, D.C.

Dear Sir:

I have the honor to transmit herewith duplicate oath of office of William B. Masterson as Office Deputy U.S. Marshal, initialed J.J.G., C.C., J.W.G., 1813-98.

Mr. Masterson commenced his official duties to-day.

Yours respectfully,

WILLIAM HENKEL

U.S. Marshal

Letters such as this are fine for those who would interpret history strictly from a bureaucratic standpoint. Fortunately, for the rest of us, a less formal, and far more human, approach was taken by the members of the press who left their breezy impressions for posterity. Typical was this account given on page 6 of the Wednesday, March 29, 1905 edition of the New York *Times:*

*Theodore Roosevelt
in 1885 at age
twenty-seven
when he first
met Bat Masterson.
Although dressed
as a Dakota
ranchman,
this picture
of Roosevelt
was taken in
New York City.
(Jack Demattos
Collection.)*

### BAT MASTERSON SWORN IN.

#### He Hopes Spring Poets and Yarn Spinners Will Quit Now.

"Bat" Masterson, the mild-mannered, quiet man about whom so many blood-curdling yarns have been spun, went down to the Post Office Building at 3 o'clock yesterday afternoon and was sworn in as a Deputy United States Marshal. There was nothing spectacular about it. He just walked into Marshal Henckel's (sic) office, was taken to Commissioner Alexander's room, and swore that he would do his duty.

Then he was made the target for half a dozen photographers, although he said he didn't like it. Last night, at the Delavan, after starting in on his fiscal year at the salary of $3,500 (sic), he said that there were other things that he didn't like.

He said he wanted to deny with as much emphasis as he knew how that he was a "bad man." When he was asked how many men he really had killed, he said "all that talk was tommy-rot,"

'This tale about notches—that's what gets next to me,' said "Bat." 'Who ever heard of a pistol having notches on it? I've seen a pistol once or twice myself—though not so often as some folks believe—and I've yet to see the first notch on the handle of one.'

'But the worst blow of all to me, it's the way the Spring poets jumped on me. I can stand all these newspaper articles about my killing Indians, and all that rot, (though they're bad enough,) but when it comes to the Spring poets writing rhymes about me I'm down and out. That's a little too much.'

'I'm goint to be a Marshal here just like any other one, I suppose. There won't be any occasion for trouble. I'll try to do my duty and I'll be glad enough to get the salary.'

'The Lord knows I haven't done anything like what's been printed. I can't say I like it much either; it seems a little like ridicule to me, and no man likes ridicule. I hope that when I turn out to be just an ordinary, two-legged man it'll let up a little.'

**WHEN BAT MASTERSON LANDS IN NEW YORK AS NEW MARSHAL.**

*"Bat"—"Now, Knick, you be good!"*
*(Cartoon from the Kansas City JOURNAL of February 7, 1905.*
*Courtesy of Joseph W. Snell.)*

*Bat Masterson at age fifty in 1903 when he began writing a regular column for the New York MORNING TELEGRAPH. (Jack DeMattos Collection.)*

# 2

# Bat and the Press

Luckily, for western buffs, the Manhattan press refused to believe that Masterson was merely "an ordinary, two-legged man." Only four days later, the New York *Times* published an interview granted by an obviously distressed Bat to a woman reporter. This interview, which has not appeared in print since its original appearance, nearly eighty years ago, offers a very rare insight into the real Bat Masterson. What follows is Zoe Anderson Norris' interview with Bat Masterson, exactly as it appeared in the New York *Times* (Section 3, page 4) of Sunday, April 2, 1905:

### "BAT" MASTERSON VINDICATED

### Woman Interviewer Gives Him "Square Deal."

It's the Simple Life that Bat Masterson has been living all this time, reports to the contrary notwithstanding. How these reports got out is the question.

It is no question, however, with Bat. He thinks he knows.

A gentle knock. The door opening discloses a tall and urbane servitor, whose counternance is scarcely discernible against the blackness of the hall.

'Mister Ahern on de 'phone, Sah,' smiles the dusky servitor.

'Tell Mr. Ahern'—some inarticulate words here out of respect to the woman reporter—'that I am not at home,' declared Mr. Masterson.

The gentle closing of the door.

'Reporter,' explained Bat, 'Wants to know whether I've done any work to-day; whether I've got a search warrant out yet for some fellow and had a shot at him. Of course,' wearily, 'you have heard of the gun?'

The reporter signified with a nod that she had heard a faint rumor.

'There ain't a single notch in that gun,' asserted he. 'Get it and show it to her.'

His wife arose.

'Which gun?' she asked.

Bat gave a gesture of utter hopelessness.

'Now ain't that just like a woman?' he demanded to know. 'Which gun? As if the woods were full of 'em.' He explained: 'I am taking care of a gun for a friend of mine in Alabama. That's the other gun she means. You can bring that, too,' in a louder voice to his wife, who had gone into the arsenal for the guns.

She brought back two guns. One was in a box; the other wasn't.

Bat took the unboxed gun and handed it courteously to the reporter. She shied off.

'Look down the muzzle of that,' said he, 'and see if it ain't an innocent looking gun.'

'But is it loaded?'

'I believe it is loaded,' nonchalantly, and turned his back while he unloaded it, explaining further; 'This is about the only way I ever unloaded a gun. Now,' handing it to her, 'ain't that as innocent a gun as you ever laid eyes on?'

**DEPUTY U. S. MARSHAL'S OATH OF OFFICE.**

FOR THE *Southern* DISTRICT OF *New York*

**1,** *William B. Masterson*, do solemnly swear that I will faithfully execute all lawful precepts directed to the **Marshal** of the *Southern* District of *New York*, under the authority of the United States, and true returns make, and in all things well and truly and without malice or partiality perform the duties of the office of Deputy United States Marshal of the *Southern* District of *New York*, during my continuance in said office, and take only my lawful fees; and that I will support and defend the Constitution of the United States against all enemies, foreign and domestic; and I will bear true faith and allegiance to the same; that I take this obligation freely, without any mental reservation or purpose of evasion; and that I will well and faithfully discharge the duties of the office upon which I am about to enter: So HELP ME GOD.

*W. B. Masterson*
*Office Deputy Marshal*

Sworn to and subscribed before me, this ___28th___ day of *March 1905*

*New York*. *March 28th, 1905*

I certify that the above-named *William B. Masterson*, Deputy Marshal, entered upon the performance of his official duties the ___28th___ day of *March 1905*

*William Henkel*
United States Marshal.

*Bat Masterson's oath of office as a deputy U.S. Marshal for the District of New York, March 1905.*

'Yes. With the cartridges on the table.'

'And do you see any notches on it?'

'Narry a notch,' said the reporter.

Bat busied himself with the box of the other, opening it. He drew out the gun.

'You see how carefully I keep this wrapped in a wash-rag and put it back in the box.

'It's my friend's gun, he repeated.

His wife then bore the two guns preciously back to the arsenal.

No report followed. On the contrary quiet reigned.

Bat and the reporter seated themselves.

'Tell me the real story of your life,' she besought him. 'I am here to refute the statements of these outrageous reporters.'

Bat smoothed out his face with both hands and commenced.

'You would have thought,' said he, 'when I was appointed to this place that I had been appointed to an Ambassadorship abroad. The telegrams that poured in on me from all parts of the country and the reporters that—'

His counternance again became crumpled.

'The reporters!' he shouted. 'Let me tell you. I telegraphed that I would arrive over the Pennsylvania Road, then I came quietly in here at the Grand Central Station, but they met me by the hundreds. By the hundreds! How they ever knew!'

A gentle knock at the door.

The black and urbane servitor.

'Mr. Martell on de 'phone, Sah,' he smiled.

'Not at home!' shrieked Bat, and it seemed that he was upon the point of tearing his hair. Only one thing prevented. In spots where it grew it had been cut so short he could not wind his fingers in it.

*A caricature of Bat
Masterson that
appeared in the New
York TIMES, on
April 2, 1905.*

"Do you see any notches in it?"

The reporter essayed to soothe.

'The President must have liked you,' she smiled, 'to give you this place.'

Her effort succeeded. Bat was pleased. His expanded counternance showed it.

'He does like me,' he assented—and really she was not surprised. A big, fine broad-shouldered, kindly fellow, with pleasant blue-gray eyes and penciled eyebrows—'and I like him. I was with him in the West a long while. Yes, Mr. Roosevelt knew me very well in the West. He would have given me a place as Marshal of the Indian Territory at $4,000 a year, but I preferred to live in New York at little more than half the salary. I like to live in New York. If it wasn't for them re—'

'New York's all right,' interrupted the woman interviewer hastily. 'There are no flies on New York even in the middle of the Summertime.'

'You'd think,' complained Bat, 'from the way they go on that I had spent all my days in the howling unwashed West when the truth of it is that for the last five years I have lived right here in these rooms overlooking Broadway.

'Yes,' triumphantly. 'right here in these rooms. O'Rourke can tell you that if you don't believe me. But these reporters! It's been two months now since I got word that Roosevelt gave me the place. I got it while I was in Hot Springs.'

'I know, two months, and we—they—those reporters,' said the interviewer, 'have been waiting breathlessly ever since for your return.'

'Breathlessly!' cried Bat. 'They are knee deep in that hall out there the livelong day. They roost in the office.'

The woman raised up her hand and coughed slighly back of it. She had sat in the office once or twice herself, if she remembered.

*Colt Single Action (Serial number 112,737) that was ordered from the Colt factory in 1885, and shipped to Bat Masterson at Dodge City, Kansas. (Earle Collection.)*

'Now, I'll tell you all about it.' She got out her pencil and pad. 'I've told it to them again and again. They have taken it all down on a pad same as you. They have taken them flash lights of me till I didn't know where I was at.'

'Afraid of the report?' soothed the interviewer, putting that down. 'Too much like the report of a gun?'

'Went off like a skyrocket,' nodded Bat. 'Stood for 'em time and again with the same old story of the gun!'

'Mister Smith on de—'

'Not at home!' cried Bat, wildly, and the interviewer waited patiently for a space until he became calm.

'Begin now. I will see that you are vindicated,' she assured him.

'When I was a boy of seventeen,' began Bat.

'He was a boy of seventeen once,' put in his wife.

'I am fifty now,' went on Bat. (you'd never think it to look at him, perhaps because of the simple life he has led.)

'I went west on a ranch. I herded buffaloes out there for a good many years. Killed 'em and sold their hides for $2.50 apiece. Made my living that way. Lived near Wichita, Kan., a long time, on a ranch. From 1871 to '74 I was with Gen. Miles hunting Indians. That was when the Indians got ostreperous, you remember.'

The interviewer jotted that down.

'Maybe you killed one or two of these Indians,' she suggested, 'and they got them mixed up with white people.'

'That might have been. I never killed a white person that I remember—might have aimed my gun at one or two in my capacity of Sheriff, but never killed one. And that's what I want you to correct. They've all got it Marshal. I never was Marshal of any town. I was Sheriff. A Sheriff,' expounding the difference, 'is elected by the people. A Marshal is appointed. The people of Dodge City elected me twice. I served both terms satisfactorily.'

'Satisfactorily,' wrote the woman.

'They've got it in Butte, too. I never was in Butte. I was pretty much everywhere else in the West, but I give you my word of honor that I never was in Butte. I never wore a pair of leggins, either. You can say that. And there's another thing I wish you would say. I never had a sombrero in my life. I never had a sombrero!'

The sombrero seemed to hurt worse than the gun. Bat's face was creased all over.

**BAT MASTER~~SON~~ ▮▮▮▮▮ ▮▮**

**He Hopes Spring Poets and Yarn Spinners Will Quit Now.**

"Bat" Masterson, the mild-mannered, quiet man about whom so many blood-curdling yarns have been spun, went down to the Post Office Building at 3 o'clock yesterday afternoon and was sworn in as a Deputy United States Marshal. There was nothing spectacular about it. He just walked into Marshal Henckel's office, was taken to Commissioner Alexander's room, and swore that he would do his duty.

Then he was made the target for a half a dozen photographers, although he said he didn't like it. Last night, at the Delavan, after starting in on his fiscal year at the salary of $3,500, he said that there were other things that he didn't like.

He said he wanted to deny with as much emphasis as he knew how that he was a "bad man." When he was asked how many men he really had killed, he said "all that talk was tommyrot."

"This tale about notches—that's what gets next to me," said "Bat." "Whoever heard of a pistol having notches on it? I've seen a pistol once or twice myself—though not so often as so~~me~~ believe—and I'~~ve~~ ~~y~~et to s~~ee a~~ notch on ~~it~~"

*A clipping from the NEW YORK TIMES, Wednesday, March 29, 1905, page 6, column 2. (Jack DeMattos photograph.)*

'Never had a sombrero,' wrote the interviewer, with the 'never' underscored, and the 'had.'

'And that's where the Cincinnati *Enquirer* did me up. Think of a paper like the Cincinnati *Enquirer*! Do you know what they did?'

The reporter signified that she was in ignorance, but she was ready not to be surprised at anything.

Bat emphasized the offense of the Cincinnati *Enquirer* with gesticulating fingers.

'They got a picture of me somehow or other,' he stormed. 'The picture had on a derby hat. Do you know what they did? They got an artist and made him take off the derby hat and put on a sombrero, the wildest, biggest!'

'Sh-h-h!' said his wife, 'Don't get excited, Bat. Really,' turning to the reporter, 'we must keep him calm.'

The knock. Mrs. Masterson hurried to the door, opened it the fraction of an inch, whispered a moment, shut it and resumed her seat.

'We must keep him calm,' she reiterated softly.

Bat had lapsed into a comatose state of suppressed indignation.

By and by the reporter aroused him with a gentle touch of her pencil.

'Sheriff of Dodge City,' she prompted.

'Sheriff of Dodge City for two years,' he responded. 'Got in a good many skirmishes during the time. Couldn't expect anything else. Bound to. Can't be avoided, but you saw for yourself there wa'n't any notches on the gun. You are the only one,' leaning forward with a smile, 'that I ever showed that gun to. You wouldn't catch me showing it to them reporters. Wouldn't gratify them that much. They'd make it a mile long and stretch pictures of it to prove it.

*A caricature of Bat Masterson that appeared in the New York TIMES of April 2, 1905.*

"Does this look like a "Bad Man?"

They'd put notches on it too, whether they were there or not.'

'In Hot Springs,' remarked his wife, 'a woman said to me, How many men is it your husband has killed anyway? A hundred?'

Bat whooped up the atmosphere with a helpless hand.

'That's the idea,' he groaned.

'The story,' prompted the reporter.

'Then,' Bat continued, 'I went to Colorado, to Denver.'

'And what did you do there?' as he hesitated.

'A good many things,' acknowledged Bat, reminiscently. 'Ran a few gambling houses. Ran a dozen poolrooms or so. Ran a boxing club. Ran a vaudeville show.'

The reporter industriously jotted down Bat's simple life on her pad.

'Cowboy, buffalo hunter, ranger, ranchman, Sheriff of Dodge City, but not of Butte; runner of gambling houses, of poolrooms, of boxing clubs, and vaudeville shows in Denver.'

And Denver's the town for the simple life. She had been there.

'Anything else?' she asked, her pencil poised.

'Yes. The livelong time, the enduring time,' making it stronger. 'I played the races. Played like an idiot too. Got the wrong tips every blooming time!'

He again became agitated. His wife put her finger to her lip. The reporter was silent.

'If I hadn't got the wrong tips,' wailed Bat, 'I wouldn't be here at the mercy of these reporters. I would be rich! Rich!'

A knock at the door.

'Mister Ahern, Mr. Martell, Mr. Smith, Mr. —,' a dozen names rolled off in the musical negro brogue, 'In de office, Sah.'

*Bat Masterson as he appeared as a gambler and sportsman in Denver, Colorado, before going to New York.*

Bat fell back helplessly in his chair.

'Why do they want to see me?' he lamented. 'I've told them the same story I've just told you. Over and over I've told it to them, and every time they come out with the same old story of the gun!'

'Never mind,' said the reporter. 'I'll write the true story of your life. I'll vindicate you. You leave that to me.'

His wife arose to say good-bye. She held out a package.

'If they won't believe Bat's lived the simple life,' said she, 'you can publish this picture of him taken at eighteen. But be careful to return it.' she added, and explained the reason why. 'It's the only proof I've got myself.' she said.

ZOE ANDERSON NORRIS

Despite Bat's protests, he remained news. The hoopla reached a fever-pitch with an incident recorded on page one of the Sunday, May 7, 1905 issue of the New York *Times*:

### $1,000 BADGE FOR MASTERSON

#### Friends Gather in Tom O'Rourke's to Honor New Deputy Marshal.

At a very early hour yesterday morning a select company gathered in the cafe of the Delavan Hotel, Broadway and Fortieth Street, to do honor to William B. ("Bat") Masterson, recently appointed Deputy United States Marshal. The ceremony took the form of a presentation of a gold badge of his new office. It was of 14-karat gold, studded with four diamonds of good size, and valued, so it was said, at $1,000.

Among those who were present and made brief speeches of appreciation of the valor and intrepidity of Marshal Masterson were Charles Prager of 14 Malden Lane, Marcus Mayer, nephew of his uncle of the same name, who lives at the Hoffman House; Tom O'Rourke of the Delavan Hotel, and William E. Lewis, to whom fell the honor of presentation.

# $1,000 BADGE FOR MASTERSON

## Friends Gather In Tom O'Rourke's to Honor New Deputy Marshal.

At a very early hour yesterday morning a select company gathered in the café of the Delevan Hotel, Broadway and Fortieth Street, to do honor to William B. ("Bat") Masterson, recently appointed Deputy United States Marshal. The ceremony took the form of a presentation of a gold badge of his new office. It was of 14-karat gold, studded with four diamonds of good size, and valued, so it was said, at $1,000.

Among those who were present and made brief speeches of appreciation of the valor and intrepidity of Marshal Masterson were Charles Prager of 14 Malden Lane, Marcus Mayer, nephew of his uncle of the same name, who lives at the Hoffman House; Tom O'Rourke of the Delevan Hotel, and William E. Lewis, to whom fell the honor of presentation.

*A clipping from the New York TIMES of Sunday, May 7, 1905, page 1, column 5. (Jack DeMattos Collection)*

*Colonel Theodore Roosevelt,*
*as commander of*
*the Rough Riders.*

# 3

# Another Gunfighter

Bat clearly regarded his appointment as a sinecure. There is no evidence that he ever showed up for work except on payday—and on those occasions, just long enough to pick up his check. In the meantime, the attempt by Roosevelt to appoint another former gunfighter, Ben Daniels, to the federal payroll had captured the public fancy and gave Bat a much-needed rest from reporters.

Benjamin Franklin Daniels was born on November 4, 1852 in LaSalle County, Illinois and went west at an early age. In 1880, Daniels was convicted of the theft of some government mules and sentenced to three years and six months in the Wyoming Penitentiary. Ben was released from prison on August 28, 1883, headed straight for Dodge City, and cultivated the friendship of Bat Masterson.

Daniels was appointed Assistant Marshal of Dodge City on July 24, 1884 and served until April 10, 1886. Five days later, Daniels shot a fellow Dodge Citian, named Ed Julian, in the back. Although it seemed to be an open and shut case of murder, Daniels was acquitted.

When the Spanish-American War broke out, Ben Daniels enlisted in Theodore Roosevelt's Rough Riders on May 21, 1898. Ben made a favorable impression on pince-nezed Theodore Roosevelt, who later recalled (*The Rough Riders*, Charles Scribner's Sons, 1899—pp. 25-26):

> Some of our best recruits came from Colorado. One, a very large, hawk-eyed man, Benjamin Franklin Daniels, had been Marshal of Dodge City when that pleasing town was probably the toughest abode of civilized man to be found anywhere on the continent.
>
> In the course of the exercise of his rather lurid functions as peace-officer he had lost half of one ear—'bitten off,' it was explained to me. Naturally he viewed the dangers of battle with philosophic calm. Such a man was, in reality, a veteran even in his first fight, and was a tower of strength to the recruits in his part of the line.

Ben survived malaria-carrying mosquitoes to return to the States as a bonafide hero of the "Splendid Little War." Daniels was present at Camp Wikoff, Long Island, on September 15, 1898, when Teddy and his Rough Riders were officially mustered out. Almost immediately, Daniels commenced what was to become a twenty-year correspondence with Roosevelt, usually seeking Teddy's influence to gain some sort of employment for himself.

Ben Daniels' wildest dreams came true on September 14, 1901 when an assassin's bullet elevated Theodore Roosevelt to the Presidency of the United States. On January 8, 1902,

*Ben Daniels in 1906 as a United States Marshal of the Arizona Territory. The fifty-four year old Daniels offered his left profile to hide his right ear that had been "chewed off." (Courtesy of the Arizona Historical Society.)*

President Roosevelt appointed Ben Daniels as United States Marshal for the Arizona Territory, subject to confirmation by the U.S. Senate.

Almost immediately, anti-Daniels telegrams began piling up in Washington. Despite the protests, Daniels was confirmed by the Senate on January 30, 1902. Within a week, the roof fell in on Ben Daniels; somehow one of Daniels' enemies found out about his old prison record and contacted the Attorney General.

By now the story had been gleefully pounced on by the press, and a minor political scandal was in the works for the Roosevelt administration. Meanwhile, the cards and letters kept coming in; an equal number either damned Daniels as a gambler, criminal, and murderer, or praised him as a lawman and war hero. But the pressure was too great; Ben Daniels formally submitted his resignation on February 25, 1902.

Despite what had happened, President Roosevelt still wanted to do something for his former Rough Rider buddy— something that didn't require Senate confirmation. Accordingly, Roosevelt had another former Rough Rider, Governor Alexander O. Brodie of Arizona, appoint Ben Daniels warden of the penitentiary at Yuma on October 1, 1904.

After three years, much of the scandal caused by Ben's first appointment as U.S. Marshal for Arizona had been forgotten, so President Roosevelt decided to try his luck a second time. On July 1, 1905, Ben Daniels became Arizona's U.S. Marshal for the second time—and, once again his confirmation

*New York's Madison Square in 1905 was Bat Masterson's neighborhood during his eighteen years as a resident. Bat's main attraction to the vicinity was the nearby Madison Square Garden.*

depended on the U.S. Senate. That confirmation would be a
long time coming; in the meantime, the Capitol Building saw an
unlikely lobbyist floating around the hallways, trying to button-
hole various senators on behalf of his friend Ben Daniels; his
name was Bat Masterson.

Bat reported his progress to President Roosevelt with the
following:

> The Raleigh
> European Plan.
> Absolutely Fire Proof.
> T.J. Talty, Manager
> Washington, D.C.
>
> December 7, 1905

To President Theodore Roosevelt
White House

My dear Mr President

Senator Fuller of Colorado will oppose the confirmation
of Ben Daniels & He stated this morning to Congressman
Towne whom I had call upon him for the purpose of having
him let up in his fight against Daniels that he could not well
do so at this time as he was being urged and petitioned by
his Colorado consituency to keep up the fight

In view of other remarks made by the senator this morning I am disposed to beleive that it is not so much  his Colorado constituency that is bothering him as it is a desire on
his part to take a slap at the President of the United States
whom he claims incorporated some good sunday school
doctrine in his message while he was appointing ex-convicts

to important federal positions & such remarks disclose a
certain degree of (illegible).

I think Mr. Towne will take the senile statesman from
the rockies in hand again and may succeed in inducing him
to say as little as he can against Ben & I imagine Ben is not
anxious to have that penitentiary matter exploited again
in the press as well as in executive session of the senate &
I am returning to New York this P.M. on 3 o'clock train
B & O

With best wishes for your health and continued success

I am most respectfully yours

W.B. MASTERSON

While Roosevelt was waiting for the Senate to take action
on Ben Daniels' confirmation, he wrote a letter to Frederic
Remington in which he compared Daniels and Masterson to
the romanticized figures Remington immortalized in oil and
bronze:

February 20, 1906

Personal

Mr. Frederic Remington,
301 Webster Avenue,
New Rochelle, N.Y.

My dear Remington:

It may be true that no white man ever understood an
Indian, but at any rate you convey the impression of understanding him! I have done what I very rarely do—that is read

a serial story—and I have followed every chapter of "The Way of an Indian" as it came out. I am very much pleased to have the inscribed volume from you now.

Is there any chance of your getting down to Washington? I should like to see you.

You know I have appointed to office in the West, and in the case of Bat Masterson, in the East, a number of the very men whose types you have permanently preserved with pencil and pen; and curiously enough, I have also appointed a few Indians to office, and one to West Point.

I have a good deal of difficulty to get the Senate to take the proper view about some of these men, notably Ben Daniels, who is really a first-class fellow.

With many thanks,

Sincerely yours,

THEODORE ROOSEVELT

Six days after sending his letter to Frederic Remington, Roosevelt received this letter of protest from a man acquainted with both Bat Masterson and Ben Daniels during their Dodge City years.

OFFICE OF D.D. ROSE, M.D.,

Physician and Surgeon

Valparaiso, Indiana
Feb. 26, 1906

My dear President,

Let me beg of you not to appoint to positions of honor and responsibility such men as Ben. Daniels and Bat. Masterson. They are both murderers.

I knew them both in Dodge City, Kan. It was the boast for Bat. Masterson that he sent twenty six of his fellow men to their graves with their boots on.

The last man killed in Dodge City, in the old days, was Ed. Julian, cowardly, sneakily shot in the back by Ben. Daniels because Julian had complained of his saloon.

Such appointments are a blot on your otherwise brilliant administration. There are plenty of honorable, clean men who would be pleased with such appointments and would be an honor, instead of a disgrace, to our beloved country.

Your most humble and obedient servant,

D.D. Rose

Despite protests of this type, Ben Daniels was at last—after more than ten agonizing months—confirmed by the United States Senate. The vote was unanimous. Ben Daniels proved to be one of the best U.S. Marshals the Arizona Territory ever had, and served out his term with distinction.

Unfortunately, the same couldn't be said about another Roosevelt appointee named Bat Masterson.

*Teddy Roosevelt's favorite photograph of himself that was taken in 1912. (Jack DeMattos Collection.)*

# 4

# Scuffles in NY

For the remainder of Theodore Roosevelt's administration, Bat Masterson continued to be a frequent, and popular, White House guest—as is apparent from this note from the President to Alfred Henry Lewis:

May 9, 1906

Mr. Alfred Henry Lewis
457 West 148th Street,
New York, N.Y.

My dear Lewis:

Many thanks for "The Throwback." I only hope I shall find it as interesting as "Sunset Trail." If so, I shall be in luck.

I had Bat down at lunch the other day.

Sincerely yours,

THEODORE ROOSEVELT

The following month Bat was back in Manhattan, where he another alleged "gunfighter" brought a touch of Dodge City-style excitement to one of the Big Apple's more posh watering holes. The story was given front-page coverage by the New York *Herald* of June 23, 1906:

## WILD WEST AT WALDORF

### Bat Masterson and Colonel Plunkett Get Belligerent

The cafe guests at the Waldorf-Astoria got a broad outline of life in a Western saloon late last night when "Bat" Masterson, United States Marshal, ran across his sometime friend, Colonel Plunkett, from Arizona. The dreaded Bat gathered himself into the cafe with blood in his eye, and he had hardly been in a moment when he spied the colonel.

'Colonel Plunkett, eh? I thought you were a friend of mine!' Bat stammered out.

Colonel Plunkett said he had not changed his opinion of the marshal, but the marshal was not in a mood to be convinced. He grabbed the colonel by the coat, and with 'Let's go outside,' started to drag Plunkett out.

Plunkett has a reputation for gunfighting that is said to be equally as brilliant as that of Masterson. But he was inclined to be submissive last night. Not so his friend E. Dinkelsheet who was sitting at a table with him before Masterson entered.

Dinkelsheet got furious when he saw Masterson grasp the Colonel by the coat. He rushed across the cafe and struck Masterson a terrific blow in the face. The Colonel was amazed at the bold stroke, and Masterson was beside himself. It was a "dead game" thing to strike "Bat" Masterson, he thought.

The next moment Dinkelsheet was sprawling on the floor from several terrific blows landed by the United States Marshal.

After that, Bat thrust his hand into his side pocket, it was said, and everybody thought there was to be a real Western scene, and jumped up at once.

The pocket was thrust against the Colonel, and then Smith, the house detective, intervened. He grabbed Masterson and invited him to get out, which he did at once. The Colonel and his friend were taken out by another door.

According to legend, a New York *World* reporter caught up with Bat at another bar and asked to see the pistol that caused the commotion at the Waldorf. At that point Bat supposedly reached in his pocket and flashed his "cannon"—a pack of cigarettes.

Less than a year later, Bat was involved in another publicized fist-fight. It seemed that Bat had been using his *Morning Telegraph* column to conduct a word-slinging duel with Walter St. Dennis, sports editor for the rival New York *Globe*. On May 17, 1907 they had an altercation at the Belmont race track  during which Bat struck St. Dennis three times. Later, Bat filed a slander suit against the *Globe* and, when the court decided in his favor, was awarded $3,500 in damages.

Theodore Roosevelt had announced his intention of not seeking a third term; this alarmed Bat—and for good reason. Once Roosevelt left office, and Bat no longer had his protection, his welfare check for "serving" as Deputy U.S. Marshal of New York would likely expire with Roosevelt's term. Bat did

*W. B. Bat Masterson
as he appeared as
the sheriff of Ford
County, Kansas
in 1877.*

his level best to get T.R. to stay on for four more years, and his
persistent efforts amused the White House press corps. Typical
was this front-page item from the Monday, April 27, 1908 issue
of the New York *Times:*

### MASTERSON AT WHITE HOUSE.

Tells the President That He Alone Can Be Elected This Fall.

WASHINGTON, April 26—"Bat" Masterson, gunfighter
and United States Deputy  Marshal of New York, was here
today, and visited the White House. The President  wel-
comed him, and the two indulged in Western yarns and
delved into politics.

Masterson could not see where any one had a chance for election next Fall except his host. He bluntly said so, and insisted that he was right. In short, he displayed the fact that he was suffering from an attack of "third termitis" in its most virulent form. The talk with "Bat" has not seemed to perturb Mr. Roosevelt to any great extent.

Bat was getting desperate; his $2000 per year deputy's salary (worth more than ten times as much in today's dollar value) went a long way in supporting his extravagant life style, as well as paying off his frequent gambling debts. Knowing that he had no friend in U.S. Marshal William Henkel, Bat bluntly asked T.R. if Henkel (or "Hinkle" as the slightly-acquainted Bat called him) could be replaced—or at least transferred to a far-off location such as the New Mexico Territory. By now, Roosevelt was on to Bat's game and didn't take the bait:

Oyster Bay, N.Y.
July 15, 1908

Mr. W.B. Masterson
c/o The Morning Telegraph
50th Street and Eighth Avenue
New York, N.Y.

My dear Masterson:

I have your letter of the 14th. My present understanding is that Marshal Hinkle (sic) is to be reappointed.

As for the New Mexican matter, that stands on a different footing. I do not know when the term of the present incumbent expires, however, and I am not quite sure as to how New Mexico would feel as to having an outsider appointed. That is something I would have to carefully consider.

Sincerely yours,

THEODORE ROOSEVELT

On February 20, 1909 White House reporters overheard the President invite Bat to be a guest at the last official affair of his administration. The event promised to be too formal for a man of Bat's simple tastes. Bat's humorous reaction to the invitation was reported in *The Santa Fe Magazine* of March, 1909 (p. 396):

### "BAT" SHOWS WHITE FEATHER

"Bat" Masterson, gun fighter, terror of the old frontier, a leader in the Grand Canyon railroad war and now deputy United States marshal in New York, showed the White feather recently, according to a New York dispatch. He fled in a panic from an evening suit and the army and navy reception in the White House. The first news his friends got of his precipitate flight was conveyed in a telegram from Baltimore.

"Bat" is a long time friend of ex-President Roosevelt, who had him come to the White House. Masterson was a guest of the president at luncheon and Mr. Roosevelt urged him to attend his last official reception tendered to the army and navy. The idea didn't appeal to the visitor.

'Nonsense,' said the president. 'You have got to come. Remember, it's my last reception. You'll come, won't you?'

'Sure,' replied "Bat," carried off his feet by the president's enthusiastic persistance. When he returned to the hotel he confided to a friend that he was as nervous as a schoolgirl and he would not go. He would telephone his decision to the president.

'Aw, forget it!' said this friend. 'You're just my build and you can have my evening clothes.'

The valet was called, the evening clothes laid out, and the friend went to attend some business, first making an engagement with "Bat" for dinner at 7:30 o'clock in a downtown hotel.

It was after 8 o'clock and the good Samaritan was mentally cursing Masterson's tardiness when a bellboy entered the cafe calling his name. The friend tore open the yellow envelope addressed to him and found therein a telegram dated at Baltimore an hour previous. It read:

'I ain't going to attend any reception. Am headed east.'

It was signed "Bat Masterson."

"*Bat Masterson, Deputy-Marshal of New York. From the January 1907 issue of HUMAN LIFE, (Courtesy of Joseph W. Snell.)*

# 5

# Out of Office

Although the new President, William Howard Taft, was Roosevelt's handpicked successor, he didn't share his predecessor's enthusiasm for gunfighters in general and Bat Masterson in particular. The beginning of the end of Bat's effortless tenure as an Office Deputy U.S. Marshal came in the form of this letter:

Department of Justice
Office of the United States
Attorney for the Southern
District of New York.

New York,
June 16, 1909.

*Personal*

Hon. George W. Wickersham,
The Attorney General.
Washington, D.C.

My dear Mr. Attorney General:

There is a matter in connection with this office which I wish to call to your attention, to wit,—one W.B. Masterson, commonly known as "Bat" Masterson, some four years ago, was appointed as a deputy marshal for the Southern District of New York, and for some reason or other, assigned to the District Attorney's office.

Whether my predecessors had any need for him or not I do not know, but I am frank to say there is no need for him now. Since the date of my appointment I have not known of his being in the office, nor performing any services in connection therewith.

I feel that I should call this matter to your attention, and I wish to be relieved from any responsibility for his assignment.

Sincerely yours,

HENRY A. WISE
U.S. Attorney

With U.S. Attorney Wise blowing the whistle on Bat's non-work "duties," the first stone was cast. Exactly a week later, it came to the attention of President William Howard Taft:

Department of Justice,
June 23, 1909.

The President,
The White House.

Dear Mr. President:

My attention has been called by the United States Attorney for the Southern District of New York to the case of

one W.B. Masterson, commonly known as "Bat" Masterson.
a deputy marshal, now receiving a salary of $2,000 per
annum. He is assigned to the District Attorney's office. Mr.
Wise writes:

'Whether my predecessors had any need for him or not I
do not know, but  I am frank to say there is no need for
him now. Since  the  date  of my appointment I have not
known of his being in the office, nor performing any services in connection therewith.'

I am advised that Mr. Masterson was appointed originally with a salary of $2,500 per annum by Executive Order.
The highest salary paid at present to a deputy marshal in
the Southern District of New York is that paid to Chief
Office Deputy Stiebling, $2,750. The next highest is $2,000
to Wm. C. Hecht. Masterson receives $2,000 and none of
the remaining twenty-four office deputies receives more
than $1,500, and only five others a salary in excess of $900.

I am advised that Masterson's employment is wholly
unnecessary to the service, and that the good of the service
would be promoted by his separation from it, and I have the
honor to ask instructions with respect to it.

Respectfully,

George W. Wickersham
Attorney General.

In order that the reader may better understand the outrage over Bat Masterson's $2,000 a year sinecure, it should be noted that the Census Bureau estimated that the average American worker of 1909 earned only $523 a year. In order to make that average figure of $523, workers had to put in a twelve hour day—six days a week! Even at that, the average worker wasn't getting by since sociologists agreed that a family needed a minimum of $800 a year, in 1909, to maintain a decent standard of living.

The effect on the morale of Bat's fellow Office Deputy Marshals can be imagined when one examines the actual salary figures for that department. Here is an actual list submitted by Charles DeWoody, examiner, to the Attorney General on April 27, 1908. The gentleman second from the bottom probably had the most appropriate name imaginable for a lawman:

| | | | |
|---|---|---|---|
| John Stiebling | age 61 | Chief Office Deputy Marshal | $2,750 |
| William C. Hecht | age 37 | Asst. Chief Office Deputy | 2,200 |
| William B. Masterson | age 53 | Office Deputy Marshal | 2,000 |
| | | | |
| Edward Doonan | age 34 | Office Deputy Marshal | 1,500 |
| Axel J. Murberg | age 39 | Office Deputy Marshal | 1,350 |
| John Kannengieser | age 33 | Office Deputy Marshal | 1,200 |
| James B. Bostwick | age 41 | Office Deputy Marshal | 1,200 |
| Lillie Henkel | age 25 | Office Deputy Marshal | 1,100 |
| Joseph J. Kumb | age 52 | Office Deputy Marshal | 1,050 |
| | | | |
| James P. Kelker | age 64 | Office Deputy Marshal | 950 |
| Lillie M. Welde | age 26 | Office Deputy Marshal | 900 |
| Henry Linicus | age 42 | Office Deputy Marshal | 900 |
| James Reed | age 39 | Office Deputy Marshal | 900 |
| William Halpin | age 63 | Office Deputy Marshal | 900 |
| John Gebhard | age 40 | Office Deputy Marshal | 900 |
| Abrah Adler | age 49 | Office Deputy Marshal | 900 |
| | | | |
| William Crawford | age 66 | Office Deputy Marshal | 850 |
| John J. Ankner | age 40 | Office Deputy Marshal | 850 |
| John W. Pinkley | age 43 | Office Deputy Marshal | 850 |
| | | | |
| Fred F. Chamberlain | age 25 | Office Deputy Marshal | 800 |
| Harry Chism | age 35 | Office Deputy Marshal | 800 |
| John Woon | age 53 | Office Deputy Marshal | 800 |
| Patrick Gilday | age 41 | Office Deputy Marshal | 800 |
| Albert J. Wirth | age 50 | Office Deputy Marshal | 800 |
| Michael F. Gunn | age 26 | Office Deputy Marshal | 800 |
| | | | |
| Peter M. Kopp | age 32 | Office Deputy Marshal | 760 |
| | | | |
| Friedrich Bernhard | age 74 | Office Deputy Marshal | 250 |

Attorney General Wickersham enclosed this list in his letter to President Taft of June 23, 1909. The President responded with this terse note:

THE WHITE HOUSE

Washington
June 29, 1909.

Hon. George W. Wickersham,
Attorney General,
Washington, D.C.

My dear Mr. Attorney General:

I have your note with respect to "Bat" Masterson, and I don't see that there is any course possible for you to pursue than to discharge him from the government employ.

Sincerely yours,

WM. H. TAFT

Having a Presidential okay to give Masterson the ax, didn't prevent the Attorney General from giving Bat one last chance— provided that Bat could be vindicated by his boss:

*Bat Masterson at age fifty-three during his term of office as Deputy U. S. Marshal for the Southern District of New York. Within a couple of years, Bat shaved off his mustache forever.*
*(Courtesy of Joseph W. Snell)*

June 30, 1909.

William Henkel, Esq.
United States Marshal,
New York, N.Y.

Sir:

I am advised by the United States Attorney that Mr. William B. Masterson, one of your office deputies, is assigned to the office of the United States Attorney; that the United States Attorney has no need of his services, and that as a matter of fact, he has not seen him in his office except on pay-day, for a considerable length of time.

You will please advise me what, if any, services Mr. Masterson performs.

Respectfully,

GEORGE W. WICKERSHAM

Attorney General.

Marshal Henkel replied to the Attorney General as follows:

Department of Justice.
Office of the United States Marshal,
Southern District of New York.
United States Court-House
Room 56, Third Floor.

New York,
July 3rd, 1909

The Attorney General, U.S.,
Department of Justice,
Washington, D.C.

Dear Sir:

I am in receipt of your letter dated June 30th, 1909, initialed C-BM, in which you state that you have been advised by the United States Attorney that William B. Masterson, one of my office deputies, is assigned to the office of the United States Attorney; that the United States Attorney has no need of his services, and that as a matter of fact, he has not seen him in his office except on pay-day, for a considerable length of time; also asking to be advised if there are any other services which Mr. Masterson performs.

In reply thereto, I beg to advise you that William B. Masterson was appointed office deputy marshal on March 28th, 1905 at the personal request of Theodore Roosevelt, then President of the United States.

At the time when his appointment was being considered by me I consulted with Henry L. Burnett, who was then United States District Attorney, and he suggested that Mr.

Masterson, when appointed, be assigned to the United
States Attorney's office to perform such services for the
United States Marshal or his office, on account of having
been assigned to the United States Attorney's office.

As Mr. Wise does not require the services of Mr. Masterson, in the United States Attorney's office, I will, if the
Department desires it, assign Mr. Masterson to some other
duties where he would come directly in under my control.
Please advise me further in this matter.

Awaiting your early reply, I am,

Yours respectfully,

WILLIAM HENKEL

U.S. Marshal.

With all this buck-passing going on, it is fitting that—at just
this point—we should once again hear from the very man who,
in effect, caused the whole mess to begin with—Alfred Henry
Lewis:

457 West 148th Street
New York City

July 4th 1909

Hon Wm H. Taft
Washington D.C.

Mr Wm B. Masterson is a deputy under Marshal Hinckle
(sic) of this district. Mr M Holds the place by the personal
suggestion of Mr Roosevelt, also he is fully fitted by age,

experience and education to discharge the duties of this office.

Letters are now passing between Mr. Wickersham and Mr Wise such (word illegible) action will be one of "economy".

It was Mr Roosevelt's wish that Mr M *be* retained. I know this from his own mouth. I myself would like to see Mr M remain though I (word illegible) think my preference should possess perculiar weight. I do not (word illegible), however, to express it since the office being a public (one) is as much my office as either Mr Wickersham's or Mr Wise's

I should think too as a citizen I am concerned for public economy as are those gentlemen.

To be frank however, I write you personally because I possess doubts as to whether or not you yourself are aware of what steps are being taken in the business and I wished to clear my mind on that point.

The affair, to be sure, is a small one from your stand point, as indeed it is from mine. It is none the less of grave importance to Mr M.

It would I think be publicly and politically better if Mr M were retained. I shall not say that such retention would be a favor to myself, as I am on no such terms of nearness to you to justify my use of that expression And yet I do not say I should not so regard it upon what statements of fact are set forth in this letter you may safely rely.

Captain Butt, who knows me well, will tell you that I seldom if ever take the trouble to misrepresent. Gov. Curry of New Mexico, a friend of Mr M for years, could give you his estimate of that gentleman, if you cared to invite it. Believe me, I remain

Sincerely yours,

ALFRED HENRY LEWIS

Despite this all-out effort by Alfred Henry Lewis, the fate of Bat Masterson's no-show job was sealed. All that remained was for one of the Attorney General's investigators to deliver the coup de grace:

Department of Justice
Washington.

July 12, 1909

Memo. for the Attorney General.

I have the honor to invite your attention to the attached letter from Marshal Henkel, Southern District of New York, regarding "Bat" Masterson, office deputy marshal at a salary of $2000 per annum.

Marshal Henkel states that if the Department so desires he will assign duties to deputy Masterson (the U.S. Attorney no longer requiring his services) so that he will be directly under his control.

The Marshal does not state, however, that he actually requires or desires the services of Mr. Masterson, and it is therefore suggested that his employment should be terminated.

I await your instruction in the premises.

Respectfully,

J.J. GLOVER

Chief, Division of Accounts

This was all the ammunition the Attorney General needed to give Bat the heave-ho. He transmitted his opinion, in no uncertain terms, to Masterson's long-suffering boss:

Department of Justice

July 12, 1909

Mr. William Henkel,
United States Marshal,
New York, N.Y.

Sir:

I have your favor of the 3rd instant, with regard to William B. Masterson, one of your office deputies.

I am perfectly aware of the manner in which Mr. Masterson came to be appointed, but what I desire to know is whether he is needed on your office staff or not. There seems to be no doubt of the fact that he has not for a long time performed any of the duties for which he was assigned.

In writing to you I did not mean to request you find something for him to do. The fact seems to be that there is no occasion for his retention in the service, and, as your office seems to be sufficiently equipped without him, I see no reason why you should make a place for him under your direct control when the needs of the service would not appear to justify it.

Unless, there, you have actual need for him, I see no reason why his retention should not be terminated.

Respectfully,

GEORGE W. WICKERSHAM

Attorney General.

All that remains to be said of Bat Masterson's four-year, four-month and four day term as Office Deputy United States Marshal for the Southern District of New York came in the form of this letter:

Department of Justice,

July 15, 1909.

William Henkel, Esq.,
U.S. Marshal,
New York.

Sir:

    Replying to yours of the 14th inst. Your recommendation that the position of Office Deputy, now held by William B. Masterson, be abolished and his services discontinued, is approved.

    You will advise Mr. Masterson that his office is abolished and his services discontinued from and after August 1st, 1909.

Respectfully,

GEORGE W. WICKERSHAM

Attorney General.

*(Left to right) William J. Burns, William A. Pinkerton, and Bat Masterson in Utica, New York in 1911. The two famous detectives and Bat met when they had been hired to promote the new Savage automatic pistol.*

Bat's contribution was to author a pamphlet, *THE TENDERFOOT'S TURN*, in which he observed:

*"If we'd had the Ten-Shot Automatic in the old days . . . a tenderfoot with a Savage Automatic and the nerve to stand his ground, could have run the worst six-shooter men the West ever saw right off the range." (Courtesy of Kansas State Historical Society.)*

*President Theodore Roosevelt in 1905.*
*(Jack DeMattos Collection.)*

# 6

# Teddy's Last Hurrah

Theodore Roosevelt had been as far away from civilization, as possible, at the time of Bat's firing, and thus was unable to lend any support to his former appointee's cause. On March 23, 1909 Roosevelt had boarded a ship in Hoboken, New Jersey and sailed off for an African safari. That expedition lasted nearly a year, followed by a tour of several European countries.

On June 18, 1910 Roosevelt returned to New York City and was given a huge parade up Fifth Avenue. It was the biggest New York celebration up to that time. Among the thousands who turned out to greet Roosevelt, was a portly sports editor from the *Morning Telegraph* named Bat Masterson.

Less than a month later, Bat made his final trip to the West to cover the July 4, 1910 heavyweight championship fight between black champion Jack Johnson and former title-holder James J. Jeffries at Reno, Nevada. Bat reported the action as Johnson pounded Jeffries into the canvas. Following the fight, race riots erupted throughout the country.

Following Jeffries' defeat, Bat—and his constant companion Alfred Henry Lewis—headed back to New York City, via a train route that would take them through Colorado and Kansas. At Trinidad, Colorado on July 13, 1910 a group photo was taken of Bat, Lewis, and seven companions at the local railroad depot. That photo revealed a Bat Masterson who had become every inch the George M. Cohan era New Yorker. The familiar derby and mustache were long gone—never to return again. In their place was a rakishly-titled pork-pie hat and a clean-shaven face.

At last Bat's train chugged into Dodge City, the site of his greatest fame, which he had not seen for nearly a quarter of a century. Bat recorded his impressions of that last visit in his *Morning Telegraph* column of July 31, 1910:

> In coming down the Arkansas Valley from Pueblo to Dodge . . . I could not help wondering at the marvelous change that had come over the country in the last twenty years. As I looked from the car window after reaching the Kansas line at Coolidge, I saw in all directions groves of trees, orchards and fields bearing abundant crops of corn, wheat and alfalfa . . . the idea that the plains of Western Kansas could ever be made fertile was something I had never dreamed of . . .
>
> But why dwell further on the subject—they are now but memories . . . Dodge City is now a thriving little country village, surrounded by a thrifty farming community. There are many oldtimers still living there and it is doubtful if they would care to live elsewhere.
>
> They are well-to-do and happy. And may they live long and continue to prosper, is my sincere wish.

Bat still had Dodge City in mind when he made his next known contact with private citizen Theodore Roosevelt. The occasion was to write Roosevelt regarding an old Dodge City crony named Michael Westernhouse Sutton:

Office of the Advertising Manager
The Morning Telegraph
Long Acre Building
Broadway, 43d and 44th Streets
New York

Dec. 21, 1911

Col. Theodore Roosevelt
The Outlook,
New York City

My dear Mr. Roosevelt:

I enclose you herewith a page of the Morning Telegraph on which you will find a letter written to me by Judge Sutton of Dodge City, Kansas. Judge Sutton, in my opinion, is one of the best posted men, politically, in the west.

He has lived in Kansas since the buffalo days and has always been a consistent and aggressive Republican. I think highly of Judge Sutton's opinion.

With best wishes for a merry Christmas and a happy new year, I am,

Sincerely yours,

W.B. MASTERSON

During the latter phase of Bat Masterson's Dodge City years, he and Mike Sutton had become bitter enemies. Obviously the passage of thirty years had healed their differences. Roosevelt's reply was short and sweet:

Dec. 23rd, 1911

Dear Bat:

That is an interesting letter from Judge Sutton. Do come and let me see you sometime.

Sincerely yours,

THEODORE ROOSEVELT

At the same time Roosevelt wrote this note, he was emerging as a key figure in a notable political movement. Many Republicans were dissatisfied with Roosevelt's successor, William Howard Taft. There was a serious party split, and several Republicans, called "Progressives" established what was dubbed the "Bull Moose" party. During 1912 Theodore Roosevelt became its standard bearer. He coined a phrase when he told reporters: "My hat is in the ring."

Before he became the official head of the Progressive Party, however, T.R. made one more stab at winning the regular Republican Convention in Chicago. Bat sent him this message on the eve of the big event—using the style of jargon he usually employed in his *Morning Telegraph* column:

William E. Lewis, Editor
The Morning Telegraph

June 1, 1912

Col. Theodore Roosevelt
Associate Editor,
The Outlook,
New York City.

My dear Colonel:

I have arranged to attend the Chicago convention to do
all I can against you, of course. Before going, however, I
would like to have a few moments talk with you and would
like for you to suggest a convenient time for me to call.

It seems to me that the only place in which you have
not slugged the bosses over the ropes is right here in New
York, but you'll get to them in time and when I see them
taking the count maybe I won't laugh.

Sincerely yours,

W.B. MASTERSON

It should go without saying that Bat was indulging in some
good-natured leg-pulling when he told Roosevelt that he would
"do all I can against you" at the upcoming convention. Obviously Bat had no intention of working against the man who
once appointed him a Deputy U.S. Marshal, to support the incumbent—who had him fired from the job. This reply to Bat's
letter was sent by Roosevelt's secretary at *Outlook Magazine:*

June 3rd, 1912

My dear Mr. Masterson:

Your letter has come to the office this morning and I think the best plan is to reply straightaway that Mr. Roosevelt could see you at the Outlook office either tomorrow morning or tomorrow afternoon before four o'clock.

Faithfully yours,

(UNSIGNED)

Secretary

The Republican Convention opened in Chicago on June 18, 1912. Roosevelt suffered a resounding defeat when incumbent President William Howard Taft was renominated by his party. The final tally was 561 votes for Taft and only 107 for Roosevelt. The White House-hungry Roosevelt now had no choice but to join the Progressive Party.

One of the first to hop on the Bull Moose bandwagon with Teddy was Bat Masterson:

Office of the Advertising Manager
The Morning Telegraph
Long Acre Building
Broadway, 43d and 44th Streets

July 9, 1912

Col. Theodore Roosevelt,
Outlook Office,
City.

My dear Colonel:

I would like to see you sometime Thursday afternoon
on what I consider a matter of more or less importance in
connection with the Progressive campaign this fall. I think I
can explain matters so that it won't be necessary to take up
more than ten minutes of your time.

If you will have your secretary indicate to me if the
time I have suggested will be convenient for you, or, if not,
fix the time for me to call, I will make it a point to be there.

Very truly yours,

W.B. MASTERSON

Whatever reply Roosevelt made to Bat was not found
among his papers. On election day, Roosevelt beat Taft by a
vote of 4,119,507 to 3,484,956. Unfortunately, Teddy was defeated in turn by the Democratic candidate, Woodrow Wilson,
who won by a wide margin of 6,293,019 votes.

The next few letters between Bat and Roosevelt dealt most-
ly with Progressive Party politics:

Office of the Advertising Manager
The Morning Telegraph
Long Acre Square
New York

March 1, 1913

Col. Theodore Roosevelt
Outlook Office,
287 Fourth Ave., City.

Dear Mr. Roosevelt:

I enclose herewith a letter from Franklin Bernard which might interest you. You will probably remember that I showed you one of Mr. Bernard's letters some time ago and you told me the next time Mr. Bernard came to the city you would like to see him.

You can read this letter at your leisure and if there are any suggestions you wish to make you can advise me of same or write to Mr. Bernard personally. Mr. Bernard is an active Bull Mooser in Colorado and a stanch supporter of yours.

With very best wishes for your good health, I am,

Sincerely yours,

W.B. MASTERSON

March 4th 1913

Dear Bat:

I am much interested in Mr. Bernard's letter, but I hard-

*Theodore Roosevelt in 1912. This photograph, taken by Charles Duprez, has been reproduced more times than any other Roosevelt photograph. (Jack DeMattos Collection.)*

ly like to advise when necessarily I cannot know all the facts.

I wish that Democratic Progressives could be taken in as well as Republicans, and I think it would be ruin for the Progressives to make an alliance with any of the old gang of the Big Steve and Archie crowd.

I wish I could answer you more definitely.

Faithfully yours,

T. ROOSEVELT


The Morning Telegraph

Sept. 1, 1913

Col. Theodore Roosevelt,
The Outlook,
287 4th Avenue
New York City.

My dear Col. Roosevelt:

I send you herewith communications which I received from Mr. Franklin Bernard this morning. Mr. Bernard seems to be having some trouble in keeping the politicians and office seekers of the Progressive party in Colorado in line.

I conclude from his letter that he would like to have you lay down the law to the Colorado Progressives.

Mr. Bernard is a sincere, conscientious worker for the Progressive cause and knowing the character of the general run of Colorado politicians as I do, I can well imagine the trouble Mr. Bernard is having in holding the Progressives together.

I'm satisfied you'll know what to do and say when you read these communications.

Very respectfully yours,

W.B. MASTERSON

September 2, 1913

Dear Bat:

In the same mail with your letter came a letter from Mr. Bernard to me. I thoroughly sympathize with Mr. Bernard's difficulties, but I do not want to lay down the law anywhere at present. I shall take the matter up with the heads of the Progressive Service.

I am just about to start for South America, and I will have to take this whole matter up when I get back in the spring.

Sincerely yours,

THEODORE ROOSEVELT

Bat Masterson in 1915 when he was sports editor for the New York MORNING TELEGRAPH. (Jack DeMattos Collection.)

# 7

# Goodbye Teddy

"I had to go," said Theodore Roosevelt of his South American expedition. "It was my last chance to be a boy." Eleven days before he departed on the ill-advised trip, he once again heard from his old friend Bat Masterson:

William E. Lewis, Editor
The Morning Telegraph

Sept. 23, 1913

Col. Theodore Roosevelt,
The Outlook,
New York City.

My dear Col. Roosevelt:

I would like to drop in before you leave for South America and pay my respects to you. If you will kindly set the day and hour for me to call I will be greatly obliged.

Sincerely yours,

W.B. MASTERSON

Whatever reply Roosevelt may have made has not been found among his papers. Roosevelt and his party of six sailed for South America on October 4, 1913. Their purpose was to collect specimens for New York City's Museum of Natural History and to map Brazil's River of Doubt.

Roosevelt's health was broken permanently by this trip. He contacted jungle fever and almost died. When he arrived back in New York on May 19, 1914, Roosevelt was thirty-five pounds lighter, and had to be assisted down the ship's gangplank. It is doubtful that Bat knew just how serious Roosevelt's condition was when he wrote this letter:

William E. Lewis
The Morning Telegraph

June 23, 1914

Col. Theodore Roosevelt
c/o The Outlook
287 4th Ave., City.

My dear Col. Roosevelt:

It would afford me great pleasure to call and see you at the office of the Outlook whenever convenient to you.

I made no effort to see you on your return from South America for the reason that I realized you would be in something of a jam with leaders of the Progressive party and well wishers generally and that your time would be fully occupied until you left for Spain.

If you will kindly let me know when to call I will regard it as a very great favor. Meanwhile I wish you the best of health and good fortune.

Sincerely yours,

W.B. MASTERSON

June 26, 1914

W.B. Masterson, Esq.
Morning Telegraph
New York City.

My dear Mr. Masterson:

Mr. Roosevelt asks me to say that if you will call at this office next Wednesday morning at ten o'clock he will be very glad to see you.

Sincerely yours,

(UNSIGNED)

Acting-Secretary
to Mr. Roosevelt.

Upon arrival for his appointment, on July 1, 1914, Masterson was informed of Roosevelt's serious illness. Bat was discreet enough to leave, and send the following letter to Roosevelt in which he played dumb on Roosevelt's actual condition:

William E. Lewis, Editor
The Morning Telegraph

July 6, 1914

Col. Theodore Roosevelt
Oyster Bay, N.Y.

My dear Col. Roosevelt:

I didn't wait to see you last Wednesday morning as I was informed by your secretary, Mr. McGrath, that you were pretty well tired out from your trip; also, that you would be quite busy with personal matters after reaching your office.

As I had nothing important to take up with you and called merely to shake you by the hand and express my gratification at your safe return from the jungle I decided to leave and wait for a more convenient time for you to see me.

I would like, however, to make an appointment with you for Wednesday, the fifteenth, at Progressive headquarters in the Forty-Second Street Building at any hour you name. Also, I would like to bring along Captain Donnelly, of Nevada, whose card I enclose herewith.

The Captain is a Western pioneer and an excellent citizen and informs me that he once met you at Reno some years ago when you spoke there and would be delighted to renew the acquaintance.

With very best wishes, I am,

Sincerely yours,

W.B. MASTERSON

No reply was found to Bat's letter and it is not known if he and Captain Donnelly kept their July 15, 1914 appointment with Roosevelt. That summer, the tragedy which would become World War I was accelerated when Germany declared war on France on August 3, 1914. Within two days, Great Britain and Russia made similar declarations against Germany and the bloodbath was on. The Christmas season of 1914 was a sad one for much of the world—including the little corner of it occupied by Bat Masterson. The reason for Bat's sadness had nothing to do with the rapidly escalating war (which still seemed very distant from our shores), but rather the death of his best friend, whose obituary was given in the New York *Times* of Thursday, December 24, 1914:

### ALFRED H. LEWIS, AUTHOR IS DEAD

Famous for His "Wolfville" Stories and "The Boss,"
a Study of Tammany Hall.

#### BEGAN CAREER AS LAWYER

While Traveler and Editor in Far West, He Gathered
Material for His Picturesque Books.

Alfred Henry Lewis, the author and newspaper man, who made the quaint, picturesque characters of the old West immortal in his "Wolfville" books, died yesterday at his home, 437 West 148th Street. He had been ill for several weeks with intestinal trouble, and his wife and brothers, William E. and Irving J. Lewis, as well as Dr. William E. Cuff, his physician, were with him to the end.

Alfred Henry Lewis was born in Cleveland, Ohio, and was in his fifty-seventh year. He was educated to be a lawyer and stood first in his class of twenty-two when examined by the Supreme Court at Columbus, Ohio, on taking his examination for the bar.

At the age of 23 he was the Prosecuting Attorney of Cleveland and at the expiration of his term spent a year in the Far West. Mr. Lewis traveled and lived in New Mexico, Arizona and Western Texas, and it was during these rambles that he met the characters he later made famous in his novels.

While in New Mexico he became editor in chief and the rest of the staff of The Mora County Pioneer. The paper was published by two printers on a hand press, and this was his first newspaper work.

Later he took charge of the Las Vegas Optic while the regular editor was unfit for duty. It is said that his first issue nearly caused a riot in the town, as he showed by the relation of one incident in his own "Confessions of a Newspaper Man." He says: 'As I cheerfully evolved these children of my fancy, a note was handed in.' It ran:

'Editor Optic—I read your paper only when I am drunk. Yours truly, Alonzo Green.'

'Writing a paragraph to the effect that Alonzo was, indubitably, from his own showing, the miscreant who had been annoying The Optic under the nom de plume of 'Constant Reader' and that the editor was glad to know his right name so that on his day off he might seek him out and beat him with a stick. I sent it in to the printers marked 'First Page. Must,' and took up the burdens of life again.'

He then went to Kansas City and began the practice of law and became a friend of many of the leading newspaper men of that city. It was this friendship that led him into writing the first of his well-known "Wolfville" stories.

Mr. Lewis was sitting one evening in the office of the

# ALFRED H. LEWIS, AUTHOR, IS DEAD

## Famous for His "Wolfville" Stories and "The Boss," a Study of Tammany Hall.

## BEGAN CAREER AS LAWYER

### While Traveler and Editor In Far West, He Gathered Material for His Picturesque Books.

Alfred Henry Lewis, the author and newspaper man, who made the quaint, picturesque characters of the old West immortal in his "Wolfville" books, died yesterday at his home, 437 West 148th Street. He had been ill for several weeks with intestinal trouble, and his wife and brothers, William E. and Irving J. Lewis, as well as Dr Will..... E. Cuff, his ph......... were the end.

*A clipping from the New York TIMES, Thursday, December 24, 1914, which reported the death of author, Alfred H. Lewis.*

city editor of The Kansas City Times when he told one of the picturesque incidents of his year's travel in the Far West. The editor suggested that he write it for his paper, and Mr. Lewis did so. The result was the creation of the "Old Cattleman" who carried the narrative in the story which was the birth of "Wolfville," and the story attracted wide attention.

Newspapers from all over the country wrote for the rights to publish his next stories. He was not paid for the first story, but for the second received $360, and decided to become an author.

In the beginning he wrote under the name of "Dan Quin," and it was not until he went to Washington as correspondent for The Kansas City Times in 1891 that he began to write under his own name.

Mr. Lewis met Col. Roosevelt in 1893, when the latter was a Civil Service Commissioner in Washington, and it is said that they immediately became close friends. Col. Roosevelt prevailed upon him to gather his "Wolfville" stories together, and these were published in book form. Col. Roosevelt edited the manuscript and the late Frederick (sic) Remington did the illustrations.

Mr. Lewis was also Washington correspondent for the Chicago Times, which was later sold to the Chicago Herald, and on this occasion he was asked to resign as Washington correspondent and become an editor of The Chicago Times-Herald. He refused, and was placed in charge of the Washington bureau of The New York Journal.

He became interested in the Thaw case and wrote several magazine articles on that subject.

One of Mr. Lewis's best-known books is "The Boss," which was the result of his close study of Tammany Hall, one of the first tasks he set himself upon coming to this city. He became intimate with the leaders of that organization, and it is said came nearer to having an intimate knowledge of Richard Croker, then the "boss" of the Hall, than any other writer.

Mr. Lewis wrote in all eighteen books. His first was "Wolfville: Episodes of Cowboy Life," and his last, published in 1913, was "Faro Nell and Her Friends."

Besides the "Wolfville" stories he wrote "Black Lion Inn," "Peggy O'Neal," "The Sunset Trail," "Confessions of a Detective," "Story of Paul Jones," "The Throwback," "When Men Grow Tall," "An American Patrician—Aaron Burr," and "Apaches of New York."


While he always missed his friend and mentor Alfred Henry Lewis, Bat was able to take some solace in the equally-close relationship he had with Alfred's brother, William Eugene Lewis (1861-1924), his boss at the *Morning Telegraph*. It was William E. Lewis who sent Bat all over the country to cover the major boxing events of the era . . . and sometimes even out of the country.

One such occasion turned up on April 5, 1915 when the 61 year-old Masterson was in Havana, Cuba covering the title fight between Jack Johnson and Jess Willard for the *Morning Telegraph*. Just prior to the fight, Bat posed for his only known newsreel film clip. The segment only lasted a few seconds—just long enough for Bat to doff his hat to the camera and replace it on his very bald head. Just a month and two days after this movie clip was made, the *Lusitania* was sunk and America edged closer towards involvement in World War I.

During the next two years, Theodore Roosevelt became an outspoken advocate of American intervention. The Wilson

White House managed to ignore the chorus led by Roosevelt until April 2, 1917 when President Wilson finally asked Congress to declare war upon Germany. One week later, Theodore Roosevelt asked President Wilson for permission to lead a Rough Rider-type regiment against the Germans in France. While Roosevelt was waiting for Wilson's reply, he got some good-natured kidding from his old friend Bat Masterson:

The Morning Telegraph
Editorial Department
W.B. Masterson

May 14, 1917

Col. Theodore Roosevelt
Metropolitan Magazine
432 Fourth Avenue,
New York City.

My dear Col. Roosevelt:

I wish you would arrange for an appointment with Tex Rickard and myself to meet you at your office when convenient.

We want to tell you how to organize your European expedition and how to win your battles when you get there. You know Tex and I are wonders in matters of this kind. Anyway, I would like to have you make a date for us.

With kindest regards, I am,

Sincerely yours,

W.B. MASTERSON

THE MORNING TELEGRAPH
EDITORIAL DEPARTMENT
W. B. MASTERSON

May 14, 1917.

Col. Theodore Roosevelt,
Metropolitan Magazine,
432 Fourth Avenue,
New York City.

My dear Col. Roosevelt:-

I wish you would arrange for an appointment with Tex Rickard and myself to meet you
at your office when convenient. We want to
tell you how to organize your European
expedition and how to win your battles when
you get there. You know Tex and I are wonders
in matters of this kind. Anyway, I would like
to have you make a date for us.

With kindest regards, I am,

Sincerely yours,

*W. B. Masterson*

A letter written by Bat to President Roosevelt in 1917.
(Courtesy of Harvard University.)

*Tex Rickard, the promoter of boxing's first million-dollar gate. He was one of Bat Masterson's honorary pall bearers at Bat's funeral in 1921. (Jack DeMattos Collection.)*

Tex Rickard was, of course, the famous boxing promoter who built the new Madison Square Garden and promoted prize fighting's first "Million Dollar Gate." Rickard was a highly colorful character whose friends included Wyatt Earp and Al Capone. When Bat Masterson died, Tex Rickard was one of his pall bearers.

May 15, 1917

Dear Mr. Masterson:

With reference to your letter of May 14th, will you call at the Metropolitan office, with Mr. Rickard at about 12 o'clock noon, Saturday next, May 19th?

Sincerely yours,

THEODORE ROOSEVELT

Thus ends the known correspondence between Bat Masterson and the twenty-sixth President of the United States. Theodore Roosevelt never got a chance to serve in World War I; President Wilson turned him down. Teddy's four sons did serve, however, and one of them, Quentin, was killed in an aerial dogfight on July 14, 1918. Roosevelt was a broken man. On January 6, 1919 he died in his sleep at the age of sixty.

*A photograph of Bat and actor William S. Hart at Bat's desk taken on October 7, 1921. Bat suffered his fatal heart attack at this desk eighteen days later. (Couresty of Bob DeArment.)*

# 8
# End of an Era

1921 was the year the "Roaring Twenties" really started to roar. Prohibition had been the law of the land since January 29, 1919—but it was already painfully apparent that the Eighteenth Amendment had not discouraged those who were determined to drink. Moreover, Mr. Volstead's act had produced bathtub gin, the speakeasy and the machine-gun toting gangster as its unwanted by-product.

1921 was the year that saw Warren G. Harding sworn in as the 29th President . . . it was the year of the first transcontinental airmail flight from San Francisco to New York . . . it was also the year that Caruso died . . . the year that race riots in Tulsa, Oklahoma killed twenty-one blacks and nine whites.

1921 was the year the state of Nevada introduced a new wrinkle in capital punishment—the gas chamber . . . it was the year that Rudolph Valentino wowed 'em at the box office with two films—*The Sheik* and *The Four Horsemen of the Apocalypse* . . . the year Sinclair Lewis topped the fiction best seller list with *Main Street* and the year that F. Scott Fitzgerald wrote *The Beautiful and the Damned* . . . the year that Eugene O'Neill's *Anna Christie* won the Pulitzer Prize . . . W.C. Fields was in the latest edition of the *Ziegfeld Follies* . . . more discriminating theater goers could see Helen Hayes in *Golden Days* or John Barrymore in *Clair de Lune*.

1921 was the year that Babe Ruth was assessed a $100 fine for speeding and given a day in jail—but the Judge let him out at 4:00 so that Ruth could get to the ball park in time for the sixth inning . . . it was the year that New York's most colorful sports editor, 67 year-old Bat Masterson of the *Morning Telegraph*, attended his last heavyweight championship fight—the so-called "Million Dollar Gate" match of July 2, 1921 in which Jack Dempsey defended—and retained—his title as the heavyweight champion of the world.

1921 was the year that movie star William S. Hart paid a visit to his old friend Bat Masterson. Hart left this account of the event in his 1929 autobiography, *My Life East and West* (p. 307):

> I had some never-to-be forgotten visits with Mr. Masterson. One day we had our picture taken together on the roof of the Telegraph Building. When we came downstairs to Mr. Masterson's office, he said:
> 'Bill, sit in my chair at my desk for one more. I want to have one taken like that.'
> I did so, and he stood beside me. Mr. Masterson was sitting in the same chair eighteen days later when he heard the last call.

*Silent screen western hero, William S. Hart (1870—1946), poses with sixty-seven year old Bat Masterson on the roof of the New York MORNING TELEGRAPH on October 7, 1921. (Jack DeMattos Collection.)*

The two photos Hart described were taken on October 7, 1921. Two days later, the *Morning Telegraph* published this tribute to Bat Masterson by his friend William S. Hart:

## BILL HART INTRODUCES A REAL—NOT REEL—HERO

### Explains that there are living two men who did the daring deeds he tries to do on screen.

In May, 1917, I was passing through the town of Dodge City, Kansas. The citizens knew I was to be on the train and had a sort of Western reception ready for me. Every man and youth of the town who owned a forty-five was allowed to strap it on—which meant that they all wore 'em.

The rector of the Catholic Church made a speech of welcome on behalf of the Mayor and gave me the freedom of the city, and then, throwing back his coat, showed he, too, had a six-shooter and cartridge belt about his waist. This he presented to me in the name of the citizens of Dodge City. It had been taken from the body of the last desperado killed on Front Street by Sheriff Chalk Benson (sic).

They then held the Overland Limited train forty minutes while they took me to the site of old Boot Hill, the cemetery where reposed the remains of evildoers killed in the upholding of the law, all of whom died and were buried with their boots on.

All this the citizens of Dodge City, Kansas did for me—to show me their appreciation of my efforts truthfully set forth upon the screen the early days of the West.

Now, I am just an actor—a mere player—seeking to reproduce the lives of those great gunmen who molded a new country for us to live in and enjoy peace and prosperity. And we have today in America two of these men with us in the flesh. It is not astounding that their deeds of heroism are not more known. The whole of our great continent separates them. One is on the Pacific, the other on the Atlantic Coast. One resides in Pasadena, Calif., the other in New York City. One is Wyatt Earp, the other William B. (Bat) Masterson.

To those few who have studied the history of frontier days, these two names are revered as none others. They are the last of the greatest band of gun-fighters—upholders of law and order—that ever lived. Wild Bill Hickok, Luke Short, Doc Holliday, Shotgun Collins, Ben Thompson, all have crossed the Big Divide but Bat Masterson and Wyatt Earp still live—and long may they do so!

It would be idle for me to attempt to set down the deeds of these two men—great writers have already done so—writers who knew and loved the West, such as Alfred Henry Lewis.

To all who like my pictures, to all who are kind enough to give me their support, I say get these books; get all the books you can setting forth the history of those days, and read them well, and then you will all realize as I do what a wonderful thing it is that we still have these two giant figures with us—not imitations like myself—but the real men.

Gentle-voiced and almost sad-faced, these men are today uncheered, while I, the imitator, the portrayer, am accorded the affection of those millions who love the West. I appreciate from my heart of hearts all the honors bestowed upon me, and in my work I do my best to be worthy; but "lest we forget," don't let us pass up those real men—those real figures—who did so much for us in bygone days.

The frontier was a big country covering thousands and thousands of miles. There were all kinds of jobs for all kinds of men. And these men fell to the lot of maintaining law and order. They did so single-handed—their only aid being a Colt gun, ever ready to speak the one grim word it knew.

As for them, they talked but little, their words sure had a peculiar force. In those days there were rival factions—for example, the Texas cowmen considered themselves superior to the Northern cowmen. There were often great battles. I have heard of one which took place in a Western Kansas town—where, when the smoke cleared away, there were seventeen silent forms stretched upon the floor of Tim Shea's dance hall.

There were sleek, palefaced gamblers, whose white shirt fronts proclaimed their prosperity. They backed their games (many of them crooked) with their lives.

There were the desperadoes, holdup men. There were actual thieves and the rudely-molded-faced dance hall owners—all gunmen—all men who knew how to handle a gun and all fearless. To enforce the law under such conditions and in such a country took the very highest order of manhood, coupled with a cool head and iron nerve.

Such men were Bat Masterson and Wyatt Earp, known · from the Mexican border to the Canadian line. They never sought trouble—they used every means at their command to avoid it, but once it came, the lawbreakers who opposed them suddenly found they were in the middle of hell with the lights out.

Let us not forget these living Americans who, when they pass on, will be remembered by hundreds of generations. For no history of the West can be written without their wonderful deeds being recorded.

William S. Hart's article got a good review from Louella Parsons, Bat's friend and co-worker at the *Morning Telegraph*. Miss Parsons would recall, in a *Morning Telegraph* article of October 30, 1921, that:

The article, unlike many of the signed contributions from film players, did not emanate from a press agent. Mr. Hart wrote every word himself. He wrote it in longhand on Waldorf-Astoria stationery. It was published verbatim October 9—exactly as it was originally written.

On Tuesday, October 25, 1921 Bat Masterson died in his *Morning Telegraph* office from a massive heart attack. All of the New York City papers devoted considerable space to coverage of Bat's passing—including the stately New York *Times*. Of all the papers that could be quoted, the most appropriate would probably be Bat's own New York *Morning Telegraph*—which gave him this front-page send-off in their issue for Wednesday, October 16, 1921:

### "BAT" MASTERSON DIES AT HIS DESK

Famous Sheriff of Dodge City, Buffalo Hunter and Indian Fighter Stricken With Heart Failure

William Barclay ("Bat") Masterson, former sheriff of Dodge City, Kan., and Deputy United States Marshal for the Southern District of New York for seven (sic) years, died suddenly at his desk in the office of The Morning Telegraph yesterday morning. Heart failure was the cause.

Mr. Masterson had been engaged as a special writer on sporting and general topics for The Morning Telegraph since 1903, and at the time of his death was secretary for the Lewis Publishing Company. He was 67 years old.

Until about two weeks ago Mr. Masterson was apparently in excellent health. He contacted a severe cold, then was confined to his apartment at 300 West Forty-ninth Street for two days. He was up and about uncomplaining and was preparing an article for the press when he died in his chair. He was alone when stricken and must have been lifeless for a quarter of an hour when discovered by his assistant.

Mr. Masterson leaves a widow, formerly Miss Emma Walters of Philadelphia, whose father was the first Union soldier of the Civil War to be buried in that city. There are no children. Mr. Masterson is survived also by a brother, Thomas Masterson, and a sister, Mrs. James Cairns, both living in Wichita, Kan.

Funeral services will be held tomorrow afternoon at Campbell's Chapel, Broadway and Sixty-sixth Street.

## Eighteen Years a New Yorker

"Bat" Masterson had a picturesque and eventful career. A typical Westerner, he was blessed with ample courage and an ability to back it up that made him instantly a favorite character when he made his appearance in the effete East, eighteen years ago. He was never given to talking much of his own exploits.

No better tribute has ever been written of him than that of the late President Theodore Roosevelt. In the foreword of Colonel Roosevelt's comprehensive volume entitled "The Winning of the West," the author said that Bat Masterson was the finest type of Western man he had ever met; that he and others like him had done more than any other influence toward cleaning up the West and making it habitable for decent persons.

## Born on Illinois Farm

Mr. Masterson was born on a farm at Fairfield, Ill. in 1854, the son of Thomas Masterson and Katherine Kirk Masterson. There were seven children in the family, and

"Bat" was 14 years old when he left Fairfield with his folk to settle at Wichita, Kansas. His mother died in March, 1908, at the old home just outside Wichita, and his father then moved into town, living to be more than ninety years old.[1]

In the old days when herds of bison roamed the great plains, young Masterson became a buffalo hunter at the age of 16. The sporadic uprising of Indian tribes made him also an Indian fighter whose reputation was second to none in that section of the country.

At the battle of Adobe Walls on the Canadian River in New Mexico, fourteen buffalo hunters stood off 300 Indians in a fusillade lasting twenty-one days, until the arrival of United States troops.[2]

"Bat" Masterson and his little band accounted for ninety Indians killed and a great many more wounded. Only one white man of the hunting party was killed and he met his death by accident. That was the lookout who was stationed on the roof. When the engagement was about to begin he fell through a hole and was shot with his own gun.[3]

The attacking force was composed of Cheyennes and Arapahoes, while not less than 3,000 other Indians watched the progress of the fighting from the surrounding hills.[4]

### Never Tasted Strong Drink

'Dobe Walls established the prowess of Mr. Masterson in the handling of lethal weapons. He was never known to take a drink of strong liqour and was always prepared for emergencies that required rapid and energetic action.[5]

When he was only 18 years old he joined Lieutenant Baldwin's civilian scouts under Colonel Nelson A. Miles, afterward a general in the regular army. He participated in the big battle of Red River, where Geronimo was the Indian leader, and some less formidable engagements.[6]

He was wounded by Sergeant King, who shot him through the hips at Sweetwater, New Mexico.[7]

When he was 21 years old Mr. Masterson, then slight and boyish-looking, was elected Sheriff of Ford County, Kansas. The county seat was Dodge City, the most disorderly spot in America. But because of the sparsely settled and outlaw-ridden condition of that section the new sheriff found himself virtually the law and order exponent of all southwestern Kansas. It was an exceedingly ticklish job, but he held it down for seven years.[8]

This period of his life furnished the material for numerous tales of the "wild and woolly" variety, some of them true enough and others invented or grossly exaggerated, according to the kind of embellishment that suited the narrator.

## Chief of Santa Fe Police

When the Santa Fe Railroad was under construction from Trinidad, Col., to Springer, then the county seat of Colfax County, New Mexico, Mr. Masterson was appointed chief of police of the Santa Fe system, more than thirty years ago. His name was then well known throughout the Southwest as a terror to the alleged "bad men" and the nemesis of outlaws.

The region between Trinidad, Col., and Ratoon (sic), N.M., was infested with gamblers, thieves and highwaymen who preyed on the several thousand railroad laborers in contruction camps. It was the duty of the chief of railroad police to protect these men, as well as the property of the Santa Fe.[9]

Later on he became City Marshal of Trinidad at $1,000 a month for a period of two years. Then he went to Tombstone as City Marshal and Tucson, Arizona, as Deputy United States Marshal, and finally to Denver, where he devoted much of his time to the business enterprise of pugilism. Mr. Masterson lived in Denver for fifteen years.[10]

## How He Left Denver

In explaining how he happened to leave there, he said to a colleague on The Morning Telegraph:

'I lived in the same house in Denver for nine years. And then the women got to voting. On one election morning I went downstairs to cast my ballot in the same old precinct, when a woman who was standing around the polls exclaimed: *I challenge that vote!*'

'I was never so surprised in my life. I didn't know the woman, couldn't recall ever having seen her before, hadn't the faintest idea why anybody should want to prevent me from exercising the prerogative of a citizen, but I said as mildly as I could: *Madam, will you please state why you challenge my vote? I have lived in this city for fifteen years, and nine years in my present domicile.*

The only answer I got was a rap across the neck with her umbrella. That was enough for me. Yes, I decided it would be best for me to dig out for Chicago.'

The droll style of the old frontiersman in telling this incident left no doubt of his covert amusement and disenchantment.

## Friends Shocked by Masterson's Death

The following telegrams of sympathy and personal regret for the death of William Barclay ("Bat") Masterson were received by The Morning Telegraph last night from Damon Runyon, of the New York American; Lou M. Houseman of Chicago, and W.A. Phelon, baseball editor of the Cincinnati Times-Star:

*Published here for the first time are stills from the only known movie film of Bat Masterson. They were taken on April 5, 1915 in Havana, Cuba, when the sixty-one year old Masterson was attending the heavyweight championship fight between Jack Johnson and Jess Willard. (Photographed from the original film which is owned by Bill Kelly of Anaheim, California.)*

New York, Oct. 25.

I offer my sincere condolences to The Morning Telegraph on the death of "Bat" Masterson. His passing is the
loss to me of a great and personal friend, and it is the loss
to the western country of one of its most splendid characters and to the nation of one of those fine, fearless men that
can be illy spared. The world of sport will miss his untiring-
ly honest writing and his constant effort to keep the game
clean. He was a magnificent man. We shall never see his like
again.

Damon Runyon,
New York American.

Chicago, Ill., Oct. 25.

Inexpressibly shocked at the news of "Bat's" death. I
know that you feel his loss poignantly. Please send a nice
bunch of roses to his bier, marking it simply *From Lou and
Emily Close,* and send me the bill. Also express our joint
condolences to his widow.

Regards,

Lou M. Houseman.

Cincinnati, O., Oct. 25.

The last link between the glorious old west and the life
of today is gone. Sportsman and prince of friends, how we
shall miss him.

W.A. Phelon.

## NOTES

1. Bat Masterson was born on November 26, 1853 in Henryville, County Rouville, Quebec Province, Canada. He was the second of seven children born to Thomas Masterson (1823-1921) and Catherine McGurk (1836-1908). Thomas Masterson moved his family from Canada in 1861. During the next decade they lived in both Illinois and Missouri. Finally, on June 6, 1871, Thomas Masterson established permanent residence on an eighty-acre farm in Grant Township, Sedgwick County, Kansas.

2. The Battle of Adobe Walls was fought in Texas—not New Mexico. Some 28 men and one woman held off about 200 Indians for five days—not the "twenty-one days" claimed in Bat's obit.

3. William Olds was the "lookout" in question. He was killed on July 1, 1874, the fifth day of the siege, when he accidently shot himself.

4. The alleged number of "3,000 other Indians" should be taken with an enormous grain of salt.

5. All available evidence suggests that Bat Masterson was a two-fisted drinker for most of his life.

6. Bat Masterson joined Lieutenant Frank D. Baldwin's detachment of scouts on August 6, 1874 then operating in the Indian Territory and the Texas Panhandle. The party made their way down the Canadian River, where they surprised a small party of hostile Indians near Chicken Creek on August 20, 1874. During the skirmish, one Indian was killed and another was wounded.

Four days later, the scouts rejoined Colonel Miles' command near the Antelope Hills. On August 30, 1874, while in the hills that bordered the Staked Plains, the scouts were attacked by two hundred and fifty warriors. The scouts held their own, until they were rescued by Miles, Cavalry. Bat

Masterson's services as a scout terminated on October 12, 1874.

Although Bat's scouting activities were a minor part of the so-called "Red River War," there is no evidence that he "participated in the big battle of Red River," and certainly none that he ever fought against Geronimo.

7. Bat Masterson was seriously wounded in a gunfight with 4th Cavalry Corporal Melvin A. King on January 24, 1876. Despite his wound, Bat managed to kill King during the Sweetwater, Texas gunfight.

8. Bat Masterson was actually 23 years-old when he was elected Sheriff of Ford County on November 6, 1877 by the narrow margin of only three votes. Bat did not serve seven years as Sheriff—just one two-year term. He was defeated for re-election on November 4, 1879 by a vote of 404 to 268.

9. The actual situation was a famous "Railroad War" between rival companies, in which Bat served as a mercenary—not as the "Chief of Santa Fe Police." Santa Fe officials had wired Bat asking him to recruit a company of men to battle a similar force employed by the Denver, Rio Grande and Western Railroad. The two companies were then contesting the right-of-way through the Royal Gorge near Pueblo, Colorado. The fact that Bat had absolutely no legal authority, didn't prevent him from raising a large company of men that included Ben Thompson. The end of Masterson's involvement came on June 12, 1879 when his forces surrendered a roundhouse they were holding at Canon City, Colorado. The war between the rival railroads was eventually settled out of court.

10. Bat Masterson was appointed City Marshal of Trinidad, Colorado on April 17, 1882 and served until April 3, 1883. His salary was $75—not $1,000—a month. Bat also never served as City Marshal of Tombstone, nor as a Deputy U.S. Marshal in Tucson.

*Bat Masterson's gave in Woodlawn Cemetery in the Bronx which shows an incorrect birth date of 1854 instead of 1853. (Courtesy of John D. Forbes, Office Manager of Woodlawn.)*

# Epilogue

There can be no doubt that Bat Masterson went out in style. The funeral services were held at Frank E. Campbell's Funeral Church, an establishment that has presided over the final rites of some of the most celebrated figures in the public eye. Their long and impressive list includes: Lex Barker, Diana Barrymore, Constance Bennett, Ralph Bunch, Eddie Condon, Joan Crawford, Tommy and Jimmy Dorsey, Judy Garland, Texas Guinan, Howard Johnson, Bert Lahr, Gertrude Lawrence, Tommy Manville, Sigmund Romberg, U Thant, Franchot Tone, Arturo Toscaninni and Rudolph Valentino.

Five hundred persons attended Bat Masterson's funeral service at Campbell's. Bat Masterson's final press notice was given in the Thursday, October 27, 1921 edition of the *Morning Telegraph*:

## EDITORS AND FRIENDS EXTOL "BAT" MASTERSON

New York Tribune and Brooklyn Eagle, Louis Seibold,
William A. Pinkerton Acclaim Worth of Man Whose
Tumultuous Life Ended Tuesday

The funeral of William Barclay ("Bat") Masterson will take place at 2 o'clock this afternoon from the Campbell Funeral Church at Broadway and Sixty-sixth Street.

Services over the body of the noted Western scout, sheriff, United States Marshal, buffalo hunter, expert on Indian fighting, apotheosis of law and order, authority of the fistic and wrestling arenas will be conducted by the Rev. Nathan A. Seagle, rector of St. Stephen's Protestant Eqiscopal Church. The burial in Woodlawn Cemetery will be private.

The honorary pallbearers will be Tex Rickard, Thomas F. O'Rourke, William E. Lewis, Damon Runyon, William Muldoon, Val J. O'Farrell, Hype Igoe, Frank J. Price, James P. Sinnott and Charles Thorley.

### Friends Express Grief

Floral pieces have been sent by the order of William S. Hart, the motion picture star, now in Los Angeles; Lou M. Houseman of Chicago; and the editorial and mechanical departments of The Morning Telegraph. Many other friends who admired "Bat" for his personality, his achievements and his estimates of men along with his cool and whimsical philosophy, have sent to the editor of The Morning Telegraph telegraphic condolences in the measure of his loss to this newspaper, on which he served as a discerning commentator for eighteen years.

### Some Editorial Tributes

Editorials from the New York Tribune and the Brooklyn Eagle of yesterday's issue are reprinted here.

### "BAT" MASTERSON
(From the N.Y. Tribune)

It is not always that the fighter's prayer, "Lord, let me die in harness," is answered. In this William Barclay (Bat)

Masterson, of The Morning Telegraph, was especially favored. He died at his desk gripping his pen with the tenacity with which he formerly clung to the hilt of his six-shooter.

Masterson, a frontier Cyrano de Bergerac in his youth, brought vigor to his Roaring Forties. When he came to write he showed directness of expression combined with little notion of veiling his dislikes. The twenty-eight notches on the weapon he had discarded when he took up the pen inspired a certain respect for Masterson's opinions.

One who knew him in the West said of him, 'Masterson improved the world considerably by the people he removed from it.' Another said, 'Masterson is most liked for his dislikes.' In New York he specialized on pugilism, a game which he knew and admired. He abominated crookedness and hypocrisy. Often in fighting them he seemed to chafe at being restricted to the use of verbal weapons.

And so the shade of "Bat" Masterson, erect in the saddle, has ridden out into the night to pick up the trail of those who knew the old West, a ghostly train that leads beyond the last frontier, where the great adventurers and warriors ride—Kit Carson, Roosevelt, Cody, Lawton, Geronimo, Sitting Bull and the rest.

The Brooklyn Eagle editorial is as follows:

## A GOOD MAN WITH A GUN

In this routine Twentieth Century an editorial office is at least as peaceful as most business headquarters. Bombs aren't set off in front of it as often as in Wall Street; it is many years since a New York editor has seen a six-shooter pointed across his desk as an agency of protest, and it is rare that unwelcome visitors have to be ejected by the police, or even by the janitor.

Such a quiet scene seems incongruous for the end of the career of the good sheriff at Dodge City when Dodge City was the toughest town in the country. Yet ten years of such labor well performed closed the days of "Bat" Masterson, who died yesterday at his desk in the office of the Morning Telegraph.

Masterson in his youth on the plains shot several bad men in the work of maintaining order and enforcing justice, his first victim being a cowboy, one of a drunken group, who killed Masterson's brother, the town marshal of Dodge City. With nine companions he stood off a party of 300 Indians in a surprise siege which lasted twenty-one days. As a lad of 18 he fought under Col Nelson A. Miles against the Indians under the famous Geronimo.

The transformation of such a frontiersman into a peaceful newspaper reporter and editor is characteristic of the ups and downs of American life. Masterson naturally became interested in pugilism and he lost all his money backing Mitchell against Corbett. To earn his living he turned his wide knowledge of fighters and other men to account and became an excellent newspaper man, first as a sporting writer and then as an editor. He had earned the peace of his later days by his earlier two-fisted support of peace in regions to which it was a stranger.

Another contributory farewell to the spirit of the veteran plainsman and familiar Broadwayite reads:

### WILLIAM BARCLAY MASTERSON
(Affectionately known as "Bat")
by William Jerome

Good-bye, Bat,
You've gone and left us flat.

You know it wasn't just like you
To do a thing like that.
But, where you've gone we know you'll find
A welcome on the mat.
You played your part—sleep on, dear heart,
Good-bye, Bat.

Good-bye, Bat,
We'll miss that mid-day chat;
The sunshine always danced around
The chair on which you sat.
With any hungry pal at all
You'd share your bit o' fat;
There's crape today along Broadway,
Good-bye, Bat.

Good-bye, Bat,
They never heard you blat
About the things you did out West—
You wasn't built like that.
That great big golden heart of yours,
It wouldn't harm a cat.
Sweet as a "gal," so long old pal,
Good-bye, Bat.

Telegrams of Sympathy

These telegrams were received over the Western Union
loop leading into The Morning Telegraph editorial rooms:

Pittsburgh, Pa., Oct. 26

I send you my best sympathy, realizing how sad you must feel about "Bat," the thousand per cent American.

Charles Dillingham.

Newark, N.J., Oct. 26

After hearing of "Bat" Masterson's death I offer condolence to wife, brother, sister, The Morning Telegraph, and all who knew the honest, straightforward, true blue man right. If he was not your friend, you could not find out. I'd almost envy the person permitted of more copious weeping, sorrow or regret than God has allowed me. May I greet him in the Great Beyond. The place will be good enough for me.

W.S. Cleveland.

Harrisburg, Pa., Oct. 26

A great shock to hear of Mr. Masterson's death. Like the real man he was he faced his maker without a whimper. A great blow to honest sports. All Harrisburg will miss his snappy and truthful writings. Consolations to family from my boys and myself.

Joe Barrett.

New York, Oct. 26

I feel a deep personal loss in "Bat" Masterson's death. May I not extend to you my sincere sympathy. I know how much you will miss him.

James P. Sinnott.

Chicago, Ill., Oct. 26

Was terribly shocked to get sad news that dear old "Bat" passed on. He was a staunch and grand friend of mine. Kindly extend to his widow my heartfelt sympathy in this, the hour of her greatest sorrow. Kindly wire me date of funeral and where from.

William A. Pinkerton.

Baltimore, Md., Oct. 26

My deepest sympathy and condolence to your paper and staff upon the loss of "Bat" Masterson, my lifelong personal friend, born upon the south bank of the Iroquois River, just over the Indiana State line, near Momence, Ill. He was a farmer, he was a soldier, he was a fearless writer. Tonight he is immortal.

Every lover of clean, honest sport in this country will miss "Bat" Masterson. His never-ceasing warfare on crookedness in boxing has been the means of saving that sport in America. I will be represented at the funeral by Jimmy Dunedin.

Skater Reynolds.

### In the Letter Mail

Louis Seibold, of the New York Herald, in a letter to the editor of The Morning Telegraph, says:

I wish you would convey to Mr. Masterson's family my sincere sympathy for their irreparable loss and my sorrow at the passing away of a manly gentleman and staunch friend.

Nellie Revell, a patient in St. Vincent's Hospital, writes:

I haven't had so great a shock since the doctor told me I may never walk again as I did when I heard of the death of your beloved friend "Bat." I cried for the first time in months. I don't know Mrs. Masterson, but I do know what a devoted, loyal husband Mr. Masterson was. I, too, admired him immensely and grieve with you and for you in the loss of anything so priceless as a friend.

J. Hoey Lawlor, motion picture art technician, of 727 Seventh Avenue, writes:

Here is one genuine "old reader" who will mourn the loss of "Bat" Masterson. I have followed his comments and writing since the Hall-Fitzsimmons contest, now near 30 years past. His dominant courage and admiration for truth will remain in the memories of spirited sportsmen for many years to come. Another master has joined the Old Timers' Hall of Fame.

Tributes of this sort were published in newspapers from coast to coast that day—but these should suffice to show the high esteem Bat was held in. In short, he may not have been the Old West's greatest gunfighter—but there is no question he was its most beloved. That is why, when the time came to inscribe his grave marker, this simple phrase—that says so much—was added:

## LOVED BY EVERYONE

On the day of Bat Masterson's funeral at Woodlawn Cemetery in the Bronx, his friend Theodore Roosevelt had been dead nearly three years—but there was one final coincidental link between the President and the Gunfighter . . .

Bat Masterson was buried on October 27, 1921—the very date that would have been Theodore Roosevelt's sixty-third birthday!

# The End

# Sources

A work of this type would seem to preclude a conventional bibliography. Obviously, there are dozens of books available on Theodore Roosevelt—but very few of them offer more than passing mention of his relationship with the various "White House Gunfighters."

The first book on the subject of Bat Masterson was *The Sunset Trail*, a 1905 novel by Alfred Henry Lewis which did not pretend to be a biography; unfortunately, Richard O'Connor's 1957 *Bat Masterson* did pretend to be a biography. For far more reliable information on Bat Masterson's pre-New York City years, the interested reader is advised to consult the following three books:

> *Bat Masterson: The Man and the Legend*
> by Robert K. DeArment
> University of Oklahoma Press, Norman, 1979

> *Famous Gun Fighters of the Western Frontier*
> by W.B. (Bat) Masterson
> Annotated and Illustrated by Jack DeMattos
> Weatherford Press, Monroe, Washington, 1982

> *Great Gunfighters of the Kansas Cowtowns, 1867-1886*
> by Nyle H. Miller and Joseph W. Snell
> University of Nebraska Press, Lincoln, 1963

It should be noted that Bat Masterson's relationship with Theodore Roosevelt is not examined, in detail, by any of the above volumes. Because of this, interested researchers may want to know exactly where this material can be found. Microfilm copies of the following letters are available from the Microtext Division, Widener Library, Harvard University, Cambridge, Massachusetts 02138:

|  |  | Reel and Series |
|---|---|---|
| October 16, 1904 | Alfred Henry Lewis to Theodore Roosevelt | 49—1 |
| October 16, 1904 | Bat Masterson to Alfred Henry Lewis | 49—1 |
| February 2, 1905 | Theodore Roosevelt to Bat Masterson | 52—1 |
| December 7, 1905 | Bat Masterson to Theodore Roosevelt | 61—1 |
| February 20, 1906 | Theodore Roosevelt to Frederic Remington | 340—2 |
| May 9, 1906 | Theodore Roosevelt to Alfred Henry Lewis | 341—2 |
| July 15, 1908 | Theodore Roosevelt to Bat Masterson | 83—1 |
| December 21, 1911 | Bat Masterson to Theodore Roosevelt | 120—1 |
| December 23, 1911 | Theodore Roosevelt to Bat Masterson | 120—1 |
| June 1, 1912 | Bat Masterson to Theodore Roosevelt | 143—1 |
| June 3, 1912 | Theodore Roosevelt to Bat Masterson | 144—1 |
| July 9, 1912 | Bat Masterson to Theodore Roosevelt | 145—1 |
| March 1, 1913 | Bat Masterson to Theodore Roosevelt | 168—1 |
| March 4, 1913 | Theodore Roosevelt to Bat Masterson | 168—1 |
| September 1, 1913 | Theodore Roosevelt to Bat Masterson | 180—1 |
| September 2, 1913 | Theodore Roosevelt to Bat Masterson | 180—1 |
| September 23, 1913 | Bat Masterson to Theodore Roosevelt | 181—1 |
| June 23, 1914 | Bat Masterson to Theodore Roosevelt | 186—1 |

| | | |
|---|---|---|
| June 26, 1914 | Theodore Roosevelt to Bat Masterson | 186—1 |
| July 6, 1914 | Bat Masterson to Theodore Roosevelt | 187—1 |
| | | |
| May 14, 1917 | Bat Masterson to Theodore Roosevelt | 223—1 |
| May 15, 1917 | Theodore Roosevelt to Bat Masterson | 223—1 |

Copies of the following letters can be obtained from the National Archives. They are part of Record Group 60 (Judicial File No. 33 S. 31, Sections 3, 5 and 6):

| | |
|---|---|
| January 26, 1905 | U.S. Marshal William Henkel to Attorney General W.H. Moody |
| March 28, 1905 | U.S. Marshal William Henkel to Attorney General W.H. Moody |
| April 27, 1908 | Charles DeWoody report to Attorney General |
| June 16, 1909 | Henry A. Wise to Attorney General George W. Wickersham |
| June 23, 1909 | Attorney General Wickersham to President Taft |
| June 29, 1909 | President Taft to Attorney General Wickersham |
| June 30, 1909 | Attorney General Wickersham to U.S. Marshal Henkel |
| July 3, 1909 | U.S. Marshal Henkel to Attorney General Wickersham |

| | |
|---|---|
| July 4, 1909 | Alfred Henry Lewis<br>to President Taft |
| July 12, 1909 | J.J. Glover<br>to Attorney General Wickersham |
| July 12, 1909 | Attorney General Wickersham<br>to U.S. Marshal Henkel |
| July 15, 1909 | Attorney General Wickersham<br>to U.S. Marshal Henkel |

Microfilm reels containing the following newspapers, cited in this book can be obtained through interlibrary loan from the following sources:

| | |
|---|---|
| New York *Times* | Tuesday, February 7, 1905 |
| New York *Times* | Wednesday, March 29, 1905 |
| New York *Times* | Sunday, April 2, 1905 |
| New York *Times* | Sunday, May 7, 1905 |
| New York *Herald* | Saturday, June 23, 1906 |
| New York *Times* | Monday, April 27, 1908 |
| New York *Morning Telegraph* | Sunday, July 31, 1910 |
| New York *Times* | Thursday, December 24, 1914 |
| New York *Morning Telegraph* | Sunday, October 9, 1921 |
| New York *Morning Telegraph* | Wednesday, October 26, 1921 |
| New York *Morning Telegraph* | Thursday, October 27, 1921 |
| New York *Morning Telegraph* | Sunday, October 30, 1921 |

# Index

# Jack DeMattos

Jack DeMattos' interest in Theodore Roosevelt's "White House Gunfighters" began with a casual visit in 1975 to Harvard University—repository for more than 100,000 letters to and from Theodore Roosevelt. Jack was hoping to find "one or two" letters between Roosevelt and one of the noted gunfighters that he befriended. It turned out that hundreds of letters between well-known and not-so-well-known gunfighters existed. Finding the three most interesting "White House Gunfighters" was no easy task since there was a large group to choose from.

That selection was made. Future books are planned to cover Pat Garrett and Ben Daniels who were appointees of President Theodore Roosevelt.

An artist by vocation and a writer by avocation, Jack De-Mattos was born in Providence, Rhode Island, on July 26, 1944. He makes his home in North Attleboro, Massachusetts, with his wife Sandi and their two children, Dawn and Greg. After Graduating from the Art Institute of Boston in 1966, Jack became a free-lance artist who attracted national attention for his caricatures drawn from life of such show business personalities as Joan Collins, Sammy Davis, Jimmy Durante, Jayne Mansfield, Mary Tyler Moore and Barbara Streisand.

Jack has authored more than sixty articles which have appeared in such publications as *True West, Frontier Times, The Tombstone Epitaph,* and *Real West.* Since 1979 he has served as Historical Consultant for *Real West* and writes and illustrates the critically acclaimed "Gunfighters of the Real West" series for that magazine. *Masterson and Roosevelt* is his second book.